Letts
EDUCATIONAL

ADVANCED
SUBSIDIARY

AS
Revision
Notes

General Studies

Authors

Andrew Collins

Martyn Groucutt

Contents

Media and communication

The nature of science

Our changing lifestyle

Science and culture

Mathematical reasoning

Progress check answers

Index

Society

The family, gender, marriage and divorce

Types

- Conventional – husband, wife, children.
- One-parent.
- Inter-generational, or extended.
- Couples living together outside marriage.
- Nuclear – 'A social group characterised by common residence, economic co-operation and reproduction. It includes adults of both sexes, at least two of whom maintain a socially approved sexual relationship and one or more children, their own or adopted, of the sexually cohabiting adults.' (Murdoch) 1949.
- Extended – essential because it contributes towards accommodation, sickness, unemployment and old age.

Family life

Life cycle:
- birth, childhood
- single adulthood
- marriage/co-habitation
- parenthood
- middle age – children leaving home
- old age.

Changes to family life

- Increasing divorce rate – 1969 Divorce Act allowed divorce on 'irretrievable breakdown of a marriage'. This has led to more one-parent families.
- Increasing life expectancy – many single-person households are made up of elderly widows.
- Greater personal control of life style – contraception freely available; abortion generally attainable, giving women more control over their lives.
- Remarriage and reconstituted families – new families created by remarriages and children from previous marriage or relationships.

Gender role changes

- Family size – decrease in the number of children.
- Marriage – a large proportion of people do not now get married.
- Life expectancy – longer life means more opportunity for women to return to work.
- Equality movement for women in the 1960s–1970s.
- Sharing tasks in the home – preparation of meals, shopping, organisation of household bills and household repairs.

Marriage and alternatives

- Number of marriages declined (459000 in 1971; 350000 in 1999).
- Cohabiting increased in the same period: why?
  - Marriage is seen as unnecessary.
  - Men and women want children but do not want a formal commitment.
  - The financial costs of a ceremony, etc.

Divorce

- A large increase in the divorce rate: why?
  - Removal of legal and financial constraints – 1984 Act reduced time restriction for a divorce, from three years to one year of marriage.
  - Changed expectations of family life – people expect to be happy.
  - Changes to women's social position giving them increased financial independence.
  - Changing social values – the stigma of divorce has now gone. Royal divorces emphasise this – people no longer stay together 'for the sake of the children'.
  - Demographic changes – early marriage led to long marriages.

Examiner's Tip

Beware of vague generalisations in a topic such as the family. There are relevant facts in the above sections which you need to know. Give the examiner the fact, then give a relevant example:

Divorce is no longer really frowned upon in society – the divorce of Prince Charles and Princess Diana shows this.

Social class

What is it?

- Many refer to 'social strata' – the **social divisions** which appear in any society.
- They have always been with us – for example, the feudal system or the caste system in India.
- Social class can be deduced by **income**, **property** or **occupation**.

The **1991 Census** divided people into:
- professionals
- managerial/technical
- skilled non-manual/skilled manual
- partly skilled
- unskilled.

- This list indicates that occupation is a major criterion of class.
- To obtain that occupation **education and qualifications** are now essential – the type of school, the type of qualifications, etc.
- Income can have a vital bearing – but is it inherited or obtained (earned by the person themselves) – i.e. is it 'old money' or 'new money'?
- Power is an important criterion – is a headteacher in a higher social class than his/her staff?

Hence social class is a difficult concept!

But there are certain facts:
- **Housing** – in 1993, 90% of professional households were owner occupied compared with 42% of unskilled manual workers.
- **Life expectancy** – those who live in the most affluent areas can expect to live up to eight years longer than those in deprived areas.
- **Social habits** – unskilled manual workers were three times more likely to smoke than those in the professional group.
- **Education** – far fewer university entrants were from the unskilled group.

Social mobility

The opportunity to move up the social ladder has increased within the UK.

- **Education** – increasing availability of further and higher education has led to increased qualifications which open previously closed occupation doors.
- **Occupations have changed** – more demand for non-manual skills, e.g. the decline of craft apprenticeships.
- The **'old school tie' network** still exists – knowing the 'right' people to 'get in'.
- **Media/entertainment stars** use **power and influence** to be socially mobile. Elton John, for example, was working class, but today????

Underclass

This is a group which is excluded from the general prosperity of the population. Why is there an 'underclass'?

- **Economic** – deprived because of a lack of employment, the changing nature of employment (e.g. part-time work), the rise of predominantly female one-parent families. Also the social services have not been given adequate resources to help the underclass.
- **Social** – the long-term unemployed, one-parent families, etc., have not been caught by the safety net of the welfare state.
- **Cross-cultural features**
  - some sociologists claim the underclass is poor because of their values (or lack of them), for example, laziness
  - some argue that governments persuade us that underclass problems are their own fault
  - some argue that the underclass exists because of the structural inequalities of society itself.

Classless society

John Major (Prime Minister 1990–1997) argued for this, claiming that equal opportunities flourish and so everyone can make of themselves what they wish. There has been levelling through:

- progressive tax system
- comparative cheapness of status symbols (e.g. foreign holidays).

BUT elements of class are still with us.

Examiner's Tip

Be clear about what the main criteria for social class are: occupation, education, income, power.

Have examples of how each of these factors determines social class.

Education

- Statutory education is from 5 to 16.
- Non-statutory education includes pre-school, as well as post-16 (that is, sixth form, further education at college, etc.)

Structure

- Children attend either primary schools (5–11) or infant (5–7) and junior (7–11) schools.
- There are still some middle schools (usually 8–12, or 9–13) where infant/primary schools feed into them.

Secondary schooling can be 11–16, then 16–18, or 11–18.

Selection

- Even between the end of World War II and the 1960s, only 20% of school pupils went to grammar schools.
- Arguments **for** selection are:
  - an élite of excellent brains to run the country
  - it stretches the most able pupils
  - like-minded pupils can be kept isolated to make rapid progress.
- Arguments **against** selection are:
  - is a test at 11 years old adequate?
  - what about those pupils who are on the margin of passing such a test?
  - what about late developers?
  - 'failures' become second-class citizens
  - those pupils who come from the most affluent homes can afford coaching
  - it divides pupils socially.

Comprehensive education

- Generally favoured by the Labour Party.
- The majority of secondary schools are comprehensive. N.B. They are now called either community schools or foundation schools.
- Some of the original precepts of comprehensive education (e.g. mixed ability teaching) no longer apply.

Schools as businesses

- Changes in education since 1988 have resulted in schools now needing to be run as a business. The main changes that have occurred are:
- National Curriculum: pupils are now divided into Key Stages.

Key Stage One:	5–7 year olds
Key Stage Two:	7–11 year olds
Key Stage Three:	11–14 year olds
Key Stage Four:	14–16 year olds.

Tests at the end of each Key Stage have led to school-by-school comparison and league tables. This has in turn led to the labelling of schools as 'good' or 'bad'.

- Local Management of Schools (LMS) means schools control their own budget.
  - The amount of budget is broadly decided by the number of pupils within the school (i.e. each pupil has a particular value in monetary terms).
  - Consequently there is a great deal of marketing and intense competition between schools in an area.
  - Falling numbers in a school can lead to staff redundancy and closure.

Private education
- In 1991, 7% of pupils attended independent schools (there are 2,000 such schools across the UK). Most pupils are from an 'upper class' background and there is considerable cost involved.
- Arguments **for** private education:
  - freedom of choice in the type of education young people undertake
  - people can use their money how they choose
  - it gives pupils a better start in life
  - the results obtained are often better
  - there are usually superior facilities and smaller class sizes.
- Arguments **against** private education:
  - it gives some an advantage over others
  - it perpetuates the class-ridden 'old school tie' system
  - the amount of money involved in those schools could be better used in a total state structure where economies of scale could then be operated.

Examiner's Tip

You will need to know about **why** and **how** we educate young people. Additionally, be clear in your own mind how schools have become far more of a business. (Think of how things have changed in your school, college, etc. Ask your staff!)

Objectivity in social science

- Social science is not an exact science.
- Natural sciences (e.g. biology) can be seen as exact sciences, because they rely on pure, unalterable facts.
- How do we make decisions? Are they made by 'free will' or are they 'determined' by society? Some argue that 'social systems' control individuals within society; others claim that individuals have the ability to exert control over their actions.

Sociology

- Sociology is seen as a social science because it was assumed that scientific methods would enable people to discover laws underlying the development of human society.
- Comte (1798–1857) believed in positivism – only directly observable facts were acceptable as evidence.

Nowadays positivism describes the approaches which reflect the methods and assumptions of the natural sciences. This includes the views of Durkheim (1858–1917) and Popper.

- Durkheim argued 'social facts are things – they can be treated in the same way as objects, events and processes of the natural worlds.' **But** because they have consciousness, humans are totally different from inanimate objects.

Inductive/deductive approach

- The **inductive** approach to sociology is **where evidence produces theories** – Durkheim's ideas.
- The **deductive** approach is to **formulate a theory** and **use information to test it** – Popper's ideas.
- There are great problems in applying this method to a study of society – society is not a laboratory where variables can be controlled, it is an open system where control is impossible.

Facts and opinions

- Sociologists collect data either by:
  - **Quantitative research** – i.e. research in the form of numbers; the numbers are necessary so that sociology can adopt scientific research measures
  - **Qualitative research** – i.e. an unstructured interview, a conversation which the sociologist evaluates later. The problem of comparison with different interviews becomes obvious.
- **Participant observation** means that the sociologist joins the group to observe the action of its members, e.g. an Ofsted inspection team.
- NB Researchers almost inevitably use a combination of both quantitative and qualitative analysis to obtain the results of a research programme.

Examiner's Tip

You do not need to have studied A Level Sociology to reach conclusions about the validity of research within social sciences. Remember:
- quantitative research
- qualitative research

and decide how conclusions are reached. You can then afford to generalise about your conclusions relating to any aspect of social sciences.

1 Why was there a large increase in the divorce rate immediately after 1945?

2 Why are there now fewer children per family?

3 Why does divorce happen more frequently in today's society?

4 Give two examples of occupations which fall into the five strata identified by the 1991 census.

5 Why do the following have an impact on perceptions of class?

   (a) Housing

   (b) Life expectancy

   (c) Social habits

   (d) Education.

6 Give reasons why social mobility is:

   (a) good

   (b) bad.

7 Why do increasing numbers of students stay on to pursue education beyond the age of 16?

8 Give reasons why schools can be seen as businesses.

9 If you wish to go to university, which factors help you make the decision?

10 How many of the factors in question 9 are 'free will' factors and how many are due to 'determinism'?

11 What information could you gain from the following statistics?

   School A   40% of pupils obtain 5 A–C grades at GCSE

   School B   20% of pupils obtain 5 A–C grades at GCSE.

Answers on page 84

Political concepts

The political system

- The UK is a **democracy**.
- The idea of a democracy comes from Ancient Greece: *demos* (people) *kratos* (power).
- 'Man is by nature a political animal' (Aristotle).
- Modern democracy is a product of the last 200 years – coming from the ideas of the American Revolution (1776–83) and the French Revolution (1789–1815). These led to the extension of the rights to vote in the UK, so that by 1928 all men and women could vote. The age restriction was reduced to 18 in 1969.
- There are other forms of government across the world:
  - **Emergent democracies**, for example the former Communist states of Eastern Europe; also the African states where the army remains an important political force.
  - **Communist states** – Cuba, Vietnam, North Korea, China – see themselves as superior to liberal democracies. They give stable government, a fairer share of the nation's wealth, freedom from unemployment, hunger and illiteracy. They do not provide freedom of choice.
  - **Military dictatorships** – the army prevents any attempt at civilian rule (for example in Burma).
  - **Nationalistic socialism** – this was identified with Hitler's Germany. Its equivalents today are states that are 'left of centre' led by a strong leader who heads the only party in the country (e.g. Saddam Hussein in Iraq, Gaddafi in Libya).

Political systems

- These grew up because representatives with similar views started to link together and form groupings which became political parties.
- Current House of Commons consists of:

Labour	418	Democratic Unionist	3
Conservative	165	SDLP	3
Liberal Democrat	46	UK Unionist Party	1
Ulster Unionist	10	Speaker	1
Scottish Nationalist	6	Sinn Fein	2
Welsh Nationalist	3	(represented but seats not taken)	

- The figures indicate the number of MPs as a result of the 1997 General Election.
- Many of the parties have agendas/policies which make them distinctive, for example the Welsh/Scottish Nationalists.
- The three major parties have a great deal of 'blurring' at the edges between them and can come across to the electorate as very similar.

- The **Conservative Party** is viewed as:
  - traditionally the party of the upper middle/middle class
  - believing in low taxation
  - holding to the freedom of the electorate to use their surplus money as they wish
  - supporting the view that there should be little interference from the state.
- The **Labour Party** on the other hand:
  - was originally the party of the working class and closely linked to the trade unions
  - traditionally believing in higher taxation particularly of the 'rich' to ensure a fairer distribution of wealth
  - held the view that the state should have a higher involvement in people's lives
  - believed that the state should control the means of production.
- The **Liberal Democrats** struggled for most of the 20th century to forge an identity for themselves. They believe in:
  - strong involvement with Europe
  - extra taxation so that it can be used on items such as health, education, etc.
  - a large element of tolerance relating to areas such as freedom of speech, etc.

Recent changes to the three main parties:

- Thatcher's victory for the Conservatives (1979) is seen as a 'sea change' in UK politics for the following reasons:
  - the sale of council houses led to a 'middle-class' feeling for new home owners
  - the Falklands War success of 1982 led to a large Conservative victory in 1983.
- The Social Democrat Party was set up by leading Labour Party members (David Owen, Shirley Williams, Roy Jenkins, for example) in the early 1980s. They eventually merged with the Liberal Party, but their defection from Labour weakened the Labour Party.
- Neil Kinnock as Labour Party leader, began to modernise the party, but there were further election defeats in 1987 and 1992. John Smith took over as leader, but died in the mid-1990s, being succeeded by Tony Blair.
- Blair's reforms included removing the Labour Party's idea for state control of the means of production; low taxation and less state interference.
- Labour won a stunning victory in the 1997 General Election.

Examiner's Tip

It is important to show that you understand what a democracy is – where individuals have freedoms such as freedom of speech, which is generated by an independent judicial system. It is also important to be able to demonstrate that you realise that other forms of government exist in other parts of the world.

(Continued next page)

The political system

Voting Trends

- The majority of the UK population are only directly involved in politics at national elections. (Even then, 25% do not register a vote.) There are a range of factors which lead people to vote for a particular political party.

- Family views (i.e. children tended to follow the voting patterns of their parents). This has changed because of:
  - increased social mobility
  - greater levels of education.

- **Class.** Traditionally, the Conservatives obtained the 'middle-class' vote and Labour the 'working-class'. Now this is far less important – for example, Labour has consistently lost manual worker votes for the last 30 years, as a decline in the manual sector of employment has occurred. There is a far greater 'service sector' workforce which, if they are 'owner-occupiers', could be more likely to vote Conservative. N.B. Labour's realisation of this and the changing of its policies were an important factor in the 1997 General Election success.

- **Gender.** Until 1979, statistically women were slightly more likely to vote Conservative. This difference has now virtually disappeared.

- **Ethnicity.** Afro-Caribbean and Asian groups are usually solidly Labour supporters. It is not clear whether support was because of the traditional link of the Labour Party with the working class, or because the party is considered more sympathetic towards ethnic minorities.

- **Youth.** Normally perceived as more radical, more likely to be left of centre and therefore vote Labour. The young were targeted by New Labour in the run up to the 1997 Election – every first-time voter received a video explaining why they should vote Labour.

- **Region.** Until the 1997 Election there was the North-South divide. Labour was strong in the North of England, Scotland and Wales. In 1997 there were no Conservative MPs returned in Scotland or Wales. The Conservatives hung on in outer London suburbs, etc., but many areas of Southern England were lost by them.

- **Policies.** Do not dominate as much as would be expected. For example, in 1987 the issues were unemployment, defence, the NHS and education. Labour were supported in those issues yet lost the election. In the 1997 election it could be argued that the main issue was to remove the Conservatives from power.

- **Leaders.** Elections in the UK are far more 'Presidential', with more 'hype' about leadership personalities. Take, for example, the comparison between Blair and Major in 1997. Blair was seen as 'cool' and 'with it', whilst Major was perceived as 'grey' and 'boring'.

- **The media** has become increasingly important. In 1979 the Conservatives used the campaign produced by the advertising company Saatchi and Saatchi, ('Let's get Britain back to work') to great effect. In 1992 *The Sun's* article 'Nightmare on Kinnock Street' led to the famous 'It was the Sun wot won it' on the day after the election. Labour noted this and Blair held long meetings with newspaper proprietors (e.g. Rupert Murdoch) to persuade them how much Labour had changed. By 1997 virtually all the national press were not advocating the Conservative Party.

- **Opinion polls** can appear to influence the electorate. People like to back winners. Polls are not always accurate. They predicted a Labour majority in 1997, but nothing like the size of the victory. Some countries ban opinion polls once an election has been called.

Examiner's Tip

It is always difficult to be sure exactly why someone votes for a particular party. The elector can fall into several of the above categories and it can be dangerous to over-classify people. Hence psephology (analysis of electoral performance) is certainly not an exact science.

Pressure groups

- These are groups which aim to influence political policy without actually seeking political power themselves. They are not like political parties because:
  - they do not put up candidates at elections
  - they are limited in scope.
- Two main types of pressure groups are:
  a) **Protective groups** brought together by:
    - a particular common interest (e.g. Surfers against Sewage)
    - common experience (e.g. Motor Neurone Disease Society)
    - a common area (e.g. Sheffield Community Association)
  b) **Promotional groups** who 'fight' for a cause in which they believe (e.g. Greenpeace, Friends of the Earth).
- Some groups can fall into both of the above categories, so an alternative categorisation could be in the form of '**insider**' or '**outsider**' groups, based on how they are treated by the government.
  - **Insider** – consulted by the government and their views are taken into account (e.g. professional teacher associations).
  - **Outsider** – far less access to the government (e.g. the Rambler's Association).
- A further division of pressure groups could be into:
  - **Permanent** – formed to protect particular interests (e.g. Alcoholics Anonymous, or the Automobile Association), or have a particular set of beliefs (e.g. the campaign for Nuclear Disarmament).
  - **Temporary** – local (e.g. campaign for a zebra crossing outside a school) or one-issue groups (e.g. the group set up to obtain justice after the death of Stephen Lawrence).

Means of operation

- Contact with MPs and political parties:
  - lobbyists are used to put the case to MPs
  - MPs are sponsored by, e.g. trade unions, company directorships.
- Gaining public support
  - use of the mass media
  - advertising
  - organising local branches to recruit members (e.g. Oxfam).
- Demonstrating levels of support
  - public demonstrations
  - petitions
  - lobbying Parliament (e.g. Rural March in London 1998).
- Providing evidence/information to decision-makers – being the source of information.
- Non-violent direct action:
  - disrupting fox hunts
  - stopping the export of calves to Europe.
- Violent protests:
  - very disorganised (e.g. the City riots of 1998)
  - very organised (e.g. the IRA – if it can be regarded as a pressure group).

Examiner's Tip

- Pressure groups are an essential part of the democratic process.
- Their influence can lead to representation in national and local politics.
- Their existence ensures that power is not monopolised by a small minority.
- With the size of the current Government's majority are pressure groups the 'real opposition' to the government?

Progress check

1 Why do you think women took so long to gain the right to vote?

2 Why do you think the age for voting was lowered to 18 in 1969?

3 How and why is it difficult to tell the differences between the two main political parties?

4 What are the advantages and disadvantages of opinion polls in the run-up to a general election?

5 Name the main attributes of a pressure group.

6 Should voting be compulsory?

7 How can the public influence the political process between elections?

Answers on page 85

Business

Employment/unemployment

- Unemployment means those who register by 'signing on' each week at their local employment office. However, there are many other elements of the population that are economically inactive:
  - women (mainly) who stay at home to look after family
  - young people under the age of 16
  - retired people
  - those in full-time further education
  - those in prison
  - those with physical/mental disability
  - those who choose not to work.
- Official definition (Labour Force Survey) of unemployment is: 'Those of working age, available for work and who have been seeking a job in the last four weeks.'

Causes of unemployment

- Historically, high rates of unemployment in 1930s were cured by the onset of war and taking on the idea of Keynesian economics (i.e. the unemployed should have cash incentives which they would spend, hence creating demand and thus job opportunities). Thatcherite monetarist ideas of the 1980s led to public sector spending being cut to control inflation, which led to increased unemployment.
- There are different forms of unemployment:
  - **Casual/seasonal** e.g. agriculture/tourism – e.g. waiters in UK seaside hotels.
  - **Structural** – the decline of the coal industry in the 1980s led to widespread unemployment, e.g. in South Wales/Nottinghamshire.
  - **Frictional** – a time gap in moving from one job to another, linked to geographical immobility.
  - **Cyclical** – during a depression demand drops (i.e. people have little spare money). This leads to production workers in luxury 'industries' being affected.
  - **Technological** – new processes such as automation or computerisation can affect the volume of people employed. This has had a great effect in the production industry in the last few decades.

Levels of unemployment

- This is a good indicator of how well the economy of a country is performing.
- Low levels of unemployment are associated with a buoyant economy.
- Politicians view levels of unemployment as the state of excess supply of labour. This is difficult to measure because the number of registered vacancies is not always accurate.

Effects of unemployment

- Personal:
  - loss of income
  - loss of purchasing power
  - loss of prestige
  - strain on family life
  - loss of standard of living.
- Local area:
  - Structural unemployment, e.g. Rover, means a great 'knock-on' effect.
  - Small firms which service major industry can be forced into liquidation and cause further unemployment.
  - Social problems – the area can appear 'depressed' resulting in a rise in crime levels, etc.
- Country:
  - Costs can be high.
  - Less income tax/National Insurance contributions paid.
  - Less VAT – therefore less purchasing power.
  - More unemployment benefits to pay out.

Examiner's Tip

You need to be able to analyse whether it is better for a government to get involved to keep firms afloat or whether market forces alone should decide if firms survive.

The costs to the economy/country generally need to be weighed against supporting inefficient economic organisations.

Leisure

- Can be defined as 'the time in which individuals are free from other social obligations'.
- Leisure and work are not mutually exclusive. For example, one person's work is another person's leisure (e.g. a council gardener).

Why has leisure time increased?

- **Longer holidays with pay.**
  Most employees expect three/four weeks paid holiday per year. This has led to more people taking a greater number of holidays each year.

- **Ageing population** – a greater percentage of the population (9.3%) is over 65. They
  - take more holidays
  - live longer
  - remain healthy/fitter for longer.

- **Shorter working week** – the hours worked per week is gradually declining. For example:

1983	37.2 hours (female)	41.5 hours (male)
1991	36.3 hours (female)	38.4 hours (male)

  N.B. There are certain groups who work longer hours (e.g. teachers, pub managers, junior doctors).

- **Greater affluence** has led to
  - more leisure breaks
  - more cars, thus greater freedom to decide where to visit.

- **Advent of motorways/by-passes.** These have led to a reduction in driving times.

Factors affecting leisure

- Age
  - Choice is shaped by the stage people have reached in their life-cycle; for example: **teenagers** 'hanging around the streets', drinking, clubbing, sports, etc.
  - Activities are chosen by the amount of spare cash they have and the lack of responsibility; for example, **over 60s** – activities can be constrained by a lack of mobility or funding. Beware of stereotypes of 'impoverished' elderly people reading and gardening!

- Work
  - Many see this as a major influence on leisure.
  - Extension pattern – work spills over into leisure time (e.g. professional occupations).
  - Neutrality pattern – leisure is a major source of life interests in contrast to unfulfilling work.
  - Opposition pattern – the activity compensates for the hazards and physical demands of dangerous jobs.
  - Sedentary occupations tend to lead to more active leisure occupations and vice versa. This can be valid, but it can also be seen as an over-simplification.

- Social class
  - Whether this is a factor is debatable.
  - If 'class' means 'high income' there is evidence (e.g. membership of a polo club).
  - Some activities cross the class divide (e.g. watching Premier League football).
  - Some activities (such as opera or ballet) remain within a certain social niche.
- Big business
  - leisure is dominated by commercial interests
  - package holidays
  - theme parks
  - pop concerts
  - cinemas
  - hotels/restaurants.
- Development of tourism, e.g.
  - Disney theme parks
  - Millennium Dome
  - Black Country Museum
  - Jorvik Museum.

Tourism

- There are several reasons why tourism is a major leisure activity:
  - the increasing pressures of modern life
  - increased education
  - the wish to experience other cultures
  - advantageous foreign exchange rates
  - the unreliability of British weather.
- Most popular destinations abroad go through several phases as tourist resorts:
  - before 'discovery' – few tourists or amenities
  - rapid increase in tourism – large increase in local employment opportunities, congestion, litter, etc.
  - continuing trend for tourists – tourists outstretch resources (water supply/sewage!): major congestion, seas polluted, increase in crime
  - unattractive to tourists – decline, leading to unemployment, closing down bars, etc.
  - decisions now needed by the government as to whether to improve matters by cleaning up beaches, building hotels, etc.

  N.B. There is an analogy here between tourists and locusts. It should not be taken too literally!

Examiner's Tip

Everyone assumes that they can answer questions on leisure. You need some facts to back up your opinions. Beware the vague generalisation which you cannot substantiate. For example, if you needed to talk about changes to a holiday area you know well, vague reminiscences of a holiday (Ibiza four years ago) will gain little credit.

Transport/location of industry

Transport

- Until 1945 the major form of transport for both freight and passengers was the railway.

- Affluence in the 1950s led to more cars and the first motorway in 1959. Better roads encouraged more use, hence less use of the railways.

- 'Beeching Axe' of the early 1960s closed down many unprofitable railway lines.

- 1970s–1980s saw a vast expansion of road transport and a proliferation of motorways. Road transport dominance started to be questioned.

- The Arab oil embargo in 1973 led to a large increase in the price of fuel and hence all goods.

- The environmental lobby began to campaign on issues such as:
  - damage to the environment by noise and atmospheric pollution
  - impact of the expanding road building programme.
  - The results of the 'Green' lobby can be seen in:
    - lead-free petrol
    - the total elimination of four-star petrol
    - less tax on lead-free petrol
    - lower road fund licences for smaller and less expensive cars.

- 1990s have seen further problems:
  - the possibility of a total 'grid lock' in major cities and on motorways
  - privatisation of railways has revealed an antiquated system in need of huge financial injections
  - hence the need for an integrated transport system, which leads to governmental problems of where to allocate resources.

Location of industry

- Originally major industries were located to minimise costs of transport and to make use of national resources (e.g. the coal and steel areas such as South Wales and Sheffield).

- The growth of motorways has led to cheap, flexible transport, hence industry can move nearer to markets.

- Government grants are relevant here: Enterprise Zones being set up has led firms to relocate. Central Government has relocated (e.g. DVLC in Swansea).

- There is a growing trend for high-tech firms to locate in areas offering more advanced technological support (e.g. M4 Silicon Valley).

- A large, well-trained workforce is not so vital today because of moves towards more capital intensive production. There is also an acceptance of commuting by the workforce.

- Firms involved in 'weight gaining' production (e.g. breweries) are usually located close to markets. 'Weight reducing' production (e.g. sawmills) have been located close to supplies.

- Some firms can be influenced by the population distribution of their potential consumers – hence locating close to densely populated areas.

- Pressure groups have affected certain industries (e.g. the Nimby attitude – Not In My Back Yard) re toxic waste, etc.

- External economies of scale can act as a stimulus for firms to base themselves in certain areas. For example, there is a supply of skilled component manufacturers in the Midlands because the UK car industry has been largely based there.

Examiner's Tip

When asked to give reasons why a business sets itself up in a particular environment, you need to bear in mind the concept of 'green belt' areas. Hence generalisations about 'in nice areas of the countryside' will not hold water, because there will always have to be a transport infrastructure to service the firm.

The workings of business and its impact on society

- Any business is an organisation which usually requires:
  - buildings
  - equipment
  - assets

  to pursue its goals.

Assets are either privately owned (private sector) or owned by the government (public sector). There are many forms of business organisation:

- Sole proprietor – typically small (e.g. plumber, hairdresser, etc.):
  - easy to establish, based on the owner's capital
  - uses the owner's labour – the one who takes the financial risk
  - competitive in the market place
  - any extra employees are the sole responsibility of the organisation
  - the owner can be made bankrupt.

- Partnership:
  - owned or run by two or more individuals
  - often with similar skills (e.g. doctors)
  - sleeping partner makes a financial contribution, but plays no active part
  - partners have to accept unlimited personal liability
  - partnerships can provide a simple way of bringing more skills and finance, leading to diversity and growth
  - they have the disadvantage of a lack of continuity as partners change, and management problems because partners have equal responsibility but not equal management expertise.

- Companies:
  - organisations with legal status and a separate identity
  - can have debts and liabilities; must be registered; can sue and be sued for breach of contract
  - most divide their financial capital funds into shares and are limited liability companies.

- Franchises: a licence issued from the franchiser to the franchisee, allowing it to sell or distribute certain brand names or products (e.g. McDonalds). Advantages of this set up to the franchiser include:
  - business expands
  - most of the effort is made by the franchisee
  - profits go to the franchiser.

  The franchisee has the benefit of:
  - trading in an already successful product
  - little difficulty in attracting customers.

Privatisation of state-controlled industries

- This has taken many forms:
  - sales of shares to transfer public corporations into public companies (e.g. British Telecom)
  - council housing sold on favourable terms to tenants
  - local services contracted to private firms (e.g. hospital cleaning).
- Advantages:
  - access to normal commercial sources of capital
  - improved business efficiency and profitability
  - reduced pressure on public funding
  - greater choice for consumers.
- Disadvantages:
  - only profitable industries are privatised and this may not be in the public interest
  - not necessarily free from government control
  - consumer choice is arguably not relevant in water/electricity supply industries.

Impact of business on society

Economic

- How much government intervention should there be in the business system?
- Employee protection (e.g. Health and Safety at Work Act – HASAWA 1974). This made employers responsible for providing safe
  - working environment
  - plant and systems of work
  - entry and exit arrangements
  - working processes (for example the Employment Protection (Consolidation) Act 1978, protects employees from unfair dismissal. To qualify, an employee must work 16 hours per week for a minimum of two years. An employer can dismiss on the grounds of incompetence; gross or serious misconduct; the post being made redundant).
- Recent legislation. Examples include the 48-hour working week rule and the 1999 Minimum Wage Act. This has the advantages of:
  - ensuring a living wage for everyone
  - ending the exploitation of weaker elements of society
  - direct comparability across the business spectrum.

  The disadvantages include:
  - minimum wage could become the maximum
  - could lead to unemployment – marginal elements being laid off
  - parts of the service industry could close completely – e.g. small seaside hotels
  - could lead to moves towards a 'black economy'.

Ecological

- Pollution problems:
  - transport causes air and noise pollution
  - pollution of rivers and beaches
  - litter and noise (the leisure industry).

(Continued next page)

The workings of business and its impact on society

Socio-cultural

- Businesses can be seen to have an obligation to help mould and achieve society's aims, for example, the sponsorship of concerts, school events, etc. This is linked to promoting an image.

- Can businesses act in a neutral way? There appears to be a great difference between the ideas of the benefits of competition and the concept of teamwork and co-operation.

- Business ethics: if firms wish to maximise profits, where do ethics fit in? For example, if a toy company produces cuddly toys and makes 100% profit, does it matter that the components are made in 'sweat shop' conditions in the Third World?

Examiner's Tip

Businesses obviously come in all shapes and sizes. Bear in mind the differences between them and also that nowadays the UK is not predominantly a manufacturing base, but is increasingly a service-led economy.

Progress check

1 Why is no unemployment an impossibility?

2 Why do you think there are more self-employed people in today's society?

3 Why are most people employed in the service/tertiary industries?

4 What have been the effects on leisure of:
   (a) longer holidays with pay
   (b) an ageing population
   (c) a shorter working week?

5 What are the problems associated with 'honeypots'?

6 Why can football no longer be seen as the 'working man's game'?

7 What are the arguments both for and against keeping railway lines open?

8 Should the rail system within the UK be improved at the expense of the road system?

9 Why is industry now more dispersed than it was a century ago?

Answers on pages 86–87

Culture and aesthetics

The idea of 'national culture'

- Some people believe there is a 'high culture' – an identity that marks a nation apart.

- One definition of national culture – a common language, religion and history.

- But in Wales there are two languages – Welsh is in the National Curriculum.

- In Scotland very few people – mainly on the islands – speak the native language, but there is a Nationalist movement, so is a common language so important?

- In Northern Ireland few people speak Gaelic, but the number is increasing. It is a powerful way of expressing Irish nationalism, wanting a united Ireland.

- The English have been accused of trying to force all parts of Britain to speak English. Does this create a 'common language'? Is there a single, or several cultures in the UK?

- In religion, a look at N. Ireland shows there is not a common religion.

- There are other examples of conflict, e.g. in Glasgow the football team Rangers are seen as the Protestant team, Celtic as the Catholic. Religion can still separate, not bind us.

- The Church of England has a privileged place in England, but this is not true in Wales, Scotland or N. Ireland. National culture is not based on religion.

- A common history? It is true that we have not been invaded since 1066 – does this help bind us?

- Other countries have had boundaries redrawn many times after wars – has this given us a sense of identity?

- When you see people singing 'Land of Hope and Glory' are they expressing part of our culture? Maybe, but how many are black, or unemployed, so is it a parody of culture?

- Think of the words, 'Wider still and wider shall thy bounds be set. God who made thee mighty, make thee mightier yet.' Is such a view acceptable?

- The world is now a global village – we can go to the other side of the world on holiday, or watch live TV broadcasts via satellite.

- The idea of the separate nation state is therefore getting harder to justify – perhaps big business is coming to dominate the world.

- Is a national identity defined by having one language, religion and history? It is certainly hard to sustain this view in the UK today.

- Economic blocs are coming to dominate the world, so will the European Union continue to grow in importance both culturally and economically?

- Is the world becoming dominated by the United States – a kind of global 'Coca-Cola capitalism' creating a world-wide culture for the young?

- Britain now contains many people from many nationalities, especially those from the former Empire. We may be a nation – but do we have a single national culture?

- Many people around the world, particularly in Germany, find it hard to understand why the British still seem fixated on the two world wars. Is it triumphalism, or clinging to former glories that have now gone?

- Do we still cling to a memory of the Empire 'upon which the Sun would never set'? Should we not be looking forward to playing a role in the new world order?

Images of culture

- We live in a country that counts many nationalities and faiths amongst its people.
- There are many more opportunities to experience a variety of what might be seen as 'cultural experiences', e.g.
  - the chance to taste styles of food from around the world
  - listening to and seeing many styles of music, dance and theatre
  - styles of dress
  - different religions and philosophies.
- Many do not give a second glance to people wearing turbans, or dreadlocks – we have accepted other cultures into our own.
- However, it would be untrue to say that the development of such cultural diversity has found universal support – racism remains unacceptably high.
- The report into the death of black teenager Stephen Lawrence concluded that high levels of institutional racism run through society, needing to be addressed by positive action, not plans and words.
- Do we still have a collective feeling of superiority from the time of the Empire?
- Is there a religious element ingrained into our thinking from the stories of missionaries who went abroad to convert the world to Christianity?
- There are laws seeking to stop racism – should people be punished because of ideas they have about people from other countries and cultures?
- Is it possible to condemn the Nazis for their treatment of Jews while tolerating hatred and persecution of black and Asian people by British racists?

Culture in the arts

- If there are difficulties in clearly defining an identifiable culture in national or racial terms, could we look to the arts – to music, literature and art?
- Shakespeare is known the world over and is thought of as being at the heart of English culture. While this is true, how many read him for fun?
- 'Shakespeare for the masses' sounds almost derogatory, yet if his writing is at the heart of our culture, why should his work not be widely read?
- Similarly, why not adopt his work to other times, places and forms, so *Romeo and Juliet* transforms into *West Side Story* by Leonard Bernstein.

Culture from experts

- 'Pure' art, theatre and music have a host of 'experts' who define and explain their own chosen form of the arts. Perhaps if it is the arts that provide our unique place in the world we need experts to interpret, or expand their area of expertise.
- Many take the view that we do need a body of arts that defines our national consciousness, even if we ourselves have only a limited knowledge.
- It is easy to parody the arts critic – a person who can spend an entire programme discussing one painting, but isn't there something profound in such a depth of analysis?
- Music, writing and art can certainly have a strong influence on the creation of identity. This could be at national level, or more local, e.g. fans of Liverpool football club singing the song, 'You'll Never Walk Alone'.

Examiner's Tip

Writers, painters and musicians play a major part in defining our culture, but these are not necessarily English. Think of artists from other parts of Britain, e.g. Robbie Burns and Dylan Thomas.

Aesthetics

- This is defined as the study of the philosophy of the arts – the process of trying to define what makes something good, beautiful or inspirational.

- People will seek out aesthetic pleasure – a visit to an art gallery, a museum, a concert or a film, for example. Why is it a rewarding experience to do such things?

- It provides an opportunity to enjoy ourselves through the arts – to feel our views and behaviour challenged and maybe to feel uplifted with a new quality to our life's experience.

- We therefore seek aesthetic pleasure because it is rewarding if not necessarily easy. If we are to be challenged we need to **think**, so it has to go beyond the superficial and easy.

- This does not mean that modern music, art, dance, etc. cannot stand up to the rigour of analysis – such an attitude suggests 'academic snobbery'.

- For example, the *Cambridge Cultural History* states that The Beatles' 'Sergeant Pepper's Lonely Hearts Club Band' album (1967), 'was the climax of their achievement. No longer simply a chaos of songs, Sergeant Pepper is a dramatic cycle, linked by the carefulness for connection and contrast unusual in anthology records … [it] goes much further, drawing in a full symphony orchestra as well as influences from Indian music and concerning itself with the expansion of self-awareness …'.

- It is therefore possible to support an aesthetic argument being made about goodness, beauty and inspiration in a piece of music, art, dance or similar by reference not only to 'classical' art, but also by reference to inspirational modern forms of the arts.

- At the same time, be wary of assuming an artistic merit where it does not exist – the 'one-hit wonders' for example. In a General Studies exam you will need to be able to put forward an argued case – not merely that you like the sound of a latest album!

- If you choose to analyse the merits of a novel, poetry, or other literature, think about the way detailed thought goes into the characters, the storyline or the use of words to create an image.

- In trying to define 'good', you must try to be analytical, not simply descriptive.

- This applies equally to painting, photography, film – analyse the beauty and appeal.

- However, the arts can also be abused – think of how the Nazis used music and theatre in their huge, choreographed rallies.

- It is for this reason that the music of the German composer Wagner has never been performed in Israel – but is such a ban still valid so long after the Second World War?

- The word 'beauty' is perhaps rather limited in its scope – other languages have words that are sometimes better at summing up our emotions.

(Continued next page)

Aesthetics

- Is what you call 'beautiful' conjuring up exactly the same feelings in someone else or is the feeling purely emotional?

- Is language itself a limiting factor when we try to find words to sum up the joy, excitement, sadness, or whatever it is we feel?

- When two people use the same word, such as 'beautiful', to describe what they are looking at, there is no way of knowing if they both feel the same.

- However, if you listen to music and think it 'cheerful', it is unlikely somebody else would think it 'mournful' – so we can make some generalisations about our feelings, even if we can't be exact.

- 'Beauty' can be seen in magnificent grandeur – New England landscapes in the fall (autumn) or Provence in the bright sunshine of high summer.

- It can also be seen in the fine and minuscule detail of a bird's plumage, or a piece of needlework – it is not based on size.

- Similarly, 'beauty' might be found in sound – the tumbling waterfall, or the mournful song of a whale.

Examiner's Tip

Remember that a discussion of aesthetics has to be based on analysis and detail – not simply 'I like the latest album by Britpop Band because it is cool'!

Progress check

1 What are the limitations on each of the three areas used to define a national British culture – common language, common religion, common history?

2 Name some of the things that have come about in recent years that makes the idea of every single nation state having its own unique national culture more difficult to sustain.

3 Give some examples of ways in which we can experience different cultures in Britain today.

4 What do we mean by institutional racism?

5 Give an example of how Shakespeare's original work has been updated or amended for modern audiences.

6 Give an example of music providing a local and popular feeling of identity.

7 Give a definition of 'aesthetics'.

8 Name an example of the misuse of music for political ends.

9 Why might we have a difficulty with words like 'beauty' when we are describing how we feel about a painting, or some other art form?

10 What should any discussion of aesthetics be based on?

Answers on page 87

Beliefs, values and morals

Religion in the UK

- Britain is primarily Christian in tradition, although in terms of regular adherents Christianity is being caught up by Islam (Muslims) in recent years.
- There have been examples of other religions in Britain for centuries – Judaism dating back to Norman times is the oldest, and the one that has probably suffered greatest persecution in historic terms.
- Large-scale immigration mainly from Commonwealth countries in Asia, Africa and the West Indies during the economic boom after 1950 saw a variety of religious groups blossom.
- Hindus, Sikhs and Muslims arrived in considerable numbers, so temples and mosques can now be found in most sizeable towns.
- People in Britain have a right to religious freedom without interference. Groups can own property, run schools and promote their views.
- The Church of England still has a unique place in England (but not in Wales, Scotland or Ireland) in our national constitution – for example, in links with the monarchy and in having seats in the House of Lords.
- The State does not directly fund any religious activity outside State occasions (such as royal weddings), but it does provide financial aid towards preserving churches of historic importance.
- It is argued that this is preserving our history and heritage, rather than promoting Christianity to the detriment of other religions.

Religion in schools

- Many of our oldest schools – especially our small village schools – were originally built by Christian groups, particularly in the 19th century.
- About one-third of schools in Britain have a link with the Christian church, although supported by funding by the local education authority, or by central government.
- In recent years other religions have started to open schools, particularly for Muslim children. The Islamia school in London is perhaps the best known.
- Between 1944 and the start of the National Curriculum in 1988 the only compulsory subject in the British curriculum was religious education.
- Today, all pupils in local authority schools have to attend a daily act of primarily Christian worship and learn religious education unless their parents request they are exempted.
- This contrasts with many other states, such as France or the United States, where it is an offence to introduce the teaching of a specific religion into the curriculum.
- On the other hand, in some primarily rural states in the US a fundamentalist Christian view has a powerful influence in schools – in Texas, for example, the theory of evolution cannot be taught because it is seen to clash with the Bible's teaching of creation.
- It is interesting to note that at a time when regular Christian church attendance is in a fairly steep decline many church schools remain popular.

Examiner's Tip

Remember that, although dominated by Christianity, other faiths have a tradition in the UK. Many children still get at least part of their education in church schools.

- There has been a continuous Christian tradition in England since 597 AD – although the former Celtic tradition in Wales, Scotland and Ireland that it eventually subsumed goes back even earlier, to Roman times.

- The national church – the Church of England – was set up by Henry VIII primarily for political reasons. He wanted to divorce his first wife who he felt would not give him a son and heir. The Pope would not agree, so Henry broke with the Roman Catholic church in 1536.

- It has been estimated that there are around 22000 different Christian groups today.

- However, the vast majority of adherents belong to one of three broad groups:
  - **Orthodox** – mainly in Eastern Europe, Russia and the Middle East
  - **Roman Catholic** – throughout the world, especially in the former colonies of Spain, Portugal and France
  - **Protestant** – throughout the world, especially in N. Europe, N. America and the former colonies of the English and Dutch.

- The most common act of worship is based on the last meal Jesus shared with his closest followers (his disciples). Jesus told them the bread and wine they shared were his body and blood.

- There is disagreement between different groups as to whether he literally meant the bread and wine had changed.

- Because there are so many Christian groups it is not easy to sum up beliefs, but most believe there is one God, who has three parts:
  - the Father, who created the universe and everything in it
  - the Son – Jesus – who came to Earth as a human to show the way back to God when humanity had become sinful
  - the Holy Spirit (or Ghost), who enters and inspires the minds of all who believe in God.

- The Bible is the holy book, in two parts – the Old Testament (the writings before the birth of Jesus), which are shared with the Jewish faith, and the New Testament, telling the story of Jesus and the early church.

- Those who believe in God and lead good lives will live with God for ever in Heaven following death.

- Some believe the Bible is the literal truth (so they reject the idea of evolution, for example, since it says God made the Earth in six days). Most believe the Old Testament is in large part an allegory – a story used as a way of getting a message across.

- One huge controversy is over the role of women. In the Bible all of Jesus's disciples were men, and in the Orthodox and Catholic tradition only men can be priests, but in the Protestant groups there are many women ministers (the equivalent of priests).

- The Church of England has recently introduced women priests and this has led to serious splits, with many leaving to join the Roman Catholic church.

- Do you think the fact that Jesus had male disciples is a reflection of society at that time, or is a God-given message about priests today?

Examiner's Tip

It is very easy to be cynical about religion if you are not a believer in a God – or to think that your brand of Christianity is the 'true' variety. However, in a General Studies exam, try to be calm and objective!

Monotheistic religions

Islam

- Islam means 'submission' to God. It originated in 622 AD in Makkah (Mecca), the birthplace of the prophet Mohammed, the last and greatest of the prophets.
- There are over 1000 million Muslims (followers of Islam) in the world, mainly in Africa, Asia and some of the southern republics of the former Soviet Union.
- Islam is thriving in Britain, but virtually all adherents are members of families who moved to Britain from Pakistan, Bangladesh or East Africa. The British Muslim population is around one million, worshipping at over 600 mosques (there were under 10 in 1960).
- Major events in the Islamic year include Ramadan (a month of fasting) and the festivals of Id al Fitr and Id al Adha.
- The Muslim holy book is the Qur'an.
- The mosque is not only the centre of worship, but in the UK also offers instruction in the Muslim way of life and also educational and welfare activities.

Judaism

- After Christianity, this is the next oldest major religion in Britain – Jews being recorded as settling in Britain at the time of the Norman Conquest.
- The Jewish community has been persecuted in many countries over at least a thousand years – it is not just something done by the Nazis.
- The first recorded pogrom (mass murder) was in York, where the Jewish community, seeking refuge in a church, were burned to death in the 12th century.
- There are two main reasons that lie behind persecution of the Jews:
  - as a race they were seen as collectively responsible for the death of Jesus
  - they were Europe's first bankers – able to lend money with interest in the Middle Ages at a time when the Christian church saw this as a sin. This caused tensions not only of philosophy, but also of economics if people could not repay debts!
- Shakespeare's play *The Merchant of Venice*, with Shylock the Jewish money lender, reflects this nicely.
- In contemporary Britain there are around 300000 Jews, of whom 200000 live in London.
- Worship is conducted in the synagogue, mainly on the Sabbath holy-day (Saturday).
- The Jewish Bible (the Old Testament, since Jews do not believe that Jesus was the Messiah – the Son of God) is divided into three parts – the law, the prophets and the writings.
- Main festivals include Rosh Hashanah (New Year), Yom Kippur (Day of Atonement) and Pesach (Passover).

The monotheistic religions

- The three religions that started in the Middle East – Christianity, Islam and Judaism – all believe there is one God, they are monotheistic.
- They also share some characteristics – a belief in the prophets of the Old Testament and the idea that in prayer the individual is speaking directly to God, for example – and also share some common geographical important sites.
- Nowhere is this more visible than in Jerusalem – a city that is central to Judaism, Islam and Christianity.

Sikhism

- Sikhism is based on the teaching of ten 'Gurus' who lived in India between the fifteenth and seventeenth centuries.
- The first and most important was Guru Nanak (1469–1539).
- The British Sikh community numbers around 300000, mainly originating in the Punjab, or coming from East Africa.
- Sikh males have uncut hair, kept neat under a turban. There are four other requirements – to carry a comb, a wrist band on the right arm, a dagger (a reminder of warrior race origins) and to wear baggy trousers.
- Temples are called 'gurdwaras' – most Sikhs attend regular Sunday service.
- The gurdwara also serves the educational, welfare and cultural needs of the community.
- Sikhs believe God is present in all human beings. In common with Hindus they believe in 'Karma' and reincarnation, with each of us having an immortal soul.

Examiner's Tip

The monotheistic religions all believe that we have one earthly life, and through faith and living a good life humans move on to eternal life in heaven.

Polytheistic religions

- These are the faiths that have a variety of gods. The main examples found in Britain today originated in southern Asia – Hinduism, Buddhism and Sikhism.

- There has been a huge increase in the British adherents to these religions over the last half-century, largely as a result of families originally from India, Pakistan or East Africa moving to this country.

- Buddhism and Hinduism, in particular, have attracted young people to the practice of meditation and inner peace. This hit the headlines when The Beatles went to India to study meditation in the 1960s.

Hinduism

- This religion is at least 4000 years old.

- The Hindu population is about 300000 strong.

- Much worship is home-based, around a small shrine with pictures or statues of gods.

- There is also communal worship in temples called Mandirs, where the singing of hymns ('bhajans') accompanied by small cymbals, tambourines and other instruments is popular.

- Dance can also be a form of worship – organised troupes perform the stories of Hindu tradition in mime and dance, combining worship and entertainment.

- The best known Hindu gods are Krishna, Rama, Ganesh and Ambamata.

- In Hindu belief there is no beginning or end – life is a cycle of creation, existing, declining and destruction, followed again by creation.

- This goes with the idea of Karma (destiny) – the human soul being reborn in another body after death (reincarnation).

- The ultimate aim, through spiritual knowledge, devotion and good works, is to break out of this cycle so that the soul becomes united with the One Soul (Brahman). This state of oneness is called Nirvana.

- There are many Hindu festivals. The best known in the UK is Diwali – the Festival of Lights – marked by lighting lamps in windows.

Buddhism

- Buddhism is a modern Western term for the teaching of Siddhartha Gautama, the Buddha, who lived in India in the sixth century BC.
- The main branches are in Japan and China (Zen) and in Tibet, Sri Lanka, Thailand and Burma.
- Buddhists do not believe there is a soul or that we have any permanent 'self'.
- We are five forces – form (the body), feelings, perceptions, emotions and consciousness. Our desires around these forces lead to reincarnation and only when we can extinguish desires for them will we reach 'Nirvana'.
- The Buddha set out the Four Noble Truths and the Noble Eightfold Path that should be followed – you can find these in any book about Buddhism.

Examiner's Tip

Polytheistic faiths believe that life is a cycle with no clear beginning or end other than for our current fleshly appearance.

Values

- It is convenient to consider our values for life in three broad areas: religious, political and social.

Religious

- Some talk as if religious values do not change, but a look at the contemporary Christian church shows many changes.
- For example, many divorced people re-marry in religious ceremonies, and there are homosexual and lesbian groups even among the clergy.
- Can it be said that religion reflects a universal truth, or does it change to reflect contemporary opinion?
- Consider capital punishment – the Ten Commandments state 'Thou shalt not kill' and Jesus was clear that taking 'an eye for an eye' is not acceptable. However, Christians have always fought in wars and many support capital punishment.
- What about a Muslim 'fatwah' – a death sentence imposed by a senior Muslim cleric that a follower would be blessed for carrying out?
- Throughout history people have used the name of God to justify all kinds of evil – but it could be argued that this represents an abuse of religion.

Political

- Many political systems claim to be based on religious values – in fact Marxism was the first to be clearly atheist.
- Marx claimed that religion was the 'opiate of the masses' – it calmed them, gave them a sense of euphoria and stopped them taking action to get rid of oppressive political systems.
- Political values are heavily influenced by the prevailing economic reality. The wealthy see things in a different way from the poor.
- Many in Britain find it hard to accept that Britain is no longer a major world power and blatant nationalism is often seen at events like sporting fixtures. This is often fanned by the tabloid press.
- Political values often deal with the relative importance of the individual in relation to that of society as a whole.
- In political shorthand – the 'right wing' view stresses the importance of freedom for individuals.
- The 'left-wing' view places greater stress on the community as a whole and the need for the individual to act for the good of the majority.
- There is more stress on pragmatism today – the idea that you find the best solution for the immediate problem, rather than have an over-riding theory that colours all actions.
- 'New Labour' reflects this – with the government encouraging private enterprise and share ownership that in a previous generation would have been seen as Conservative policies.

Social

- Social values affect the way we behave towards other people. People sometimes talk about declining social values – often referring to sexual behaviour.
- On the other hand it could be argued that relationships are much more honest and open today than in the past.
- In Victorian cities it has been estimated that one woman in eight was a prostitute of some kind – many being visited by respectable middle-class men who put their wives on a pedestal.

Examiner's Tip

Some people say religion is at the heart of our values, others that it is economics – but in reality we get our ideas of 'good' and 'bad' from many sources.

Influences on social values

Religion

- The teachings and holy books of all religions have a lot to say about social values.
- People belonging to a particular religion will certainly try to reflect these in their lives, but they are not always binding if other pressures to act differently are powerful.
- For example, many European and North American Catholic women go against the church's view that contraception is morally wrong.

The family

- Our parents and close family are powerful forces in teaching us what is 'right' and 'wrong' – this is called socialisation.
- From early childhood we hope to learn in an environment of love, warmth, comfort and food, which provide extremely strong bases for supporting our learning.
- The immediate environment in which we live will also have an effect – life on the top floor of a tower block will be very different from life on a country estate!

Popular culture

- Often boosted by the power of the media – pop stars, sports personalities and others are often seen as role models.
- Some parents and older people express great concern about the drug culture as a negative aspect of pop culture.
- On the other hand campaigns such as 'Kick racism out of soccer' have a positive impact in promoting equality.

- Our values and the way we view the world are therefore formed through a variety of influences on us throughout our lives.
- They may not necessarily be fixed and unchanging – many people say that some event in their lives has changed the way they look at the world.
- There are important elements about our social values – the way we look at the world – that might easily appear on a General Studies exam paper, e.g.
  - can breaking the law be morally justified?
  - how far should we go to stand up for what we believe in?
  - should we always bow to the majority?
  - is it right to inform on a friend who has broken the law?
- Questions such as these do not have a 'right' or 'wrong' answer – your answer will be coloured by your own social values.

Examiner's Tip

You should always seek to explain your viewpoint in a rational way, but always remember that there might be different perspectives on the same issue. Where appropriate, acknowledge that other views do exist.

Progress check

1 Apart from Christianity, which is the longest-standing religious community in the UK?

2 Which church has a privileged place within the framework of formal English society?

3 What is Islamia?

4 Which Christian group is dominant in Eastern Europe and Russia?

5 Why do many Christians believe that priests should all be male?

6 Which religion has Makkah as a holy city?

7 What happens during the month-long period of Ramadan?

8 What is the name of the Jewish holy day?

9 With which religion do you associate Krishna, Rama and Ganesh?

10 By what name is Siddhartha Gautama better known?

11 What religion originated with the teaching of Guru Nanak?

12 Which is the only political system that is based on atheism?

13 What freedom does someone with right-wing political views seek to maximise?

14 Which campaign in soccer is trying to promote racial equality?

15 What name is given to the process of learning about the world from our immediate family?

Answers on page 88

Creativity and innovation

Important literature of the twentieth century

- There has been a wide variety of literature written over the last 100 years. Some writers had a profound effect on the thinking of their day – for example, the War Poets.
- Important books of the twentieth century range from children's classics, to political allegory; from books originally considered obscene, to feminist classics.
- Students will be able to add to the list provided – particularly writings from the latter part of the century with which you might be more familiar from your personal reading.

Important books of the twentieth century

Year	Author	Title	Notes
1902	Beatrix Potter	*The Tale of Peter Rabbit*	Animals as people (anthropomorphism)
1904	J.M. Barrie	*Peter Pan*	All royalties still go to the Great Ormond Street Hospital
1904	Anton Checkov	*The Cherry Orchard*	A play popular in its original Russian and then translated into English
1908	Kenneth Grahame	*The Wind in the Willows*	Again, animals as people
1913	D.H. Lawrence	*Sons and Lovers*	When first published, this was declared obscene and all copies destroyed
1915	D.H. Lawrence	*The Rainbow*	
1920	Agatha Christie	*The Mysterious Affair at Styles*	Her first novel introduced Hercule Poirot. Reflected post-war escapism
1922	James Joyce	*Ulysses*	This was a major step forward in the development of the novel
1926	A.A. Milne	*Winnie the Pooh*	More animals as people!
1929	Ernest Hemingway	*A Farewell to Arms*	Powerful political writing
1929	Robert Graves	*Goodbye to All That*	Autobiographical experiences of World War I
1929	W.H. Auden	*Poems* (his first collection of poetry)	Major influence on poetry of the century
1932	Aldous Huxley	*Brave New World*	Science fiction which gave warning for future societies
1933	Vera Brittain	*Testament of Youth*	World War I from a woman's perspective
1937	J.R.R. Tolkein	*The Hobbit*	
1945	George Orwell	*Animal Farm*	Satire on the development of the Soviet Union
1947	Tennessee Williams	*A Streetcar Named Desire*	Has been called the 'best play ever written by an American'

Year	Author	Title	Notes
1949	Simone de Beavoir	*The Second Sex*	One of the classic texts of modern feminism
1949	George Orwell	*1984*	Originally titled *The Last Man in Europe* – this was a warning about dictatorship
1953	Arthur Miller	*The Crucible*	Allegorical denunciation of the McCarthy purges in the USA
1956	John Osborne	*Look Back in Anger*	This play is about one of the original 'Angry Young Men'
1957	Boris Pasternak	*Dr Zhivago*	
1958	Harold Pinter	*The Birthday Party*	
1960	Stan Barstow	*A Kind of Loving*	One of the first to popularise novels on the brutality of working-class life
1967	Nell Dunn	*Poor Cow*	Female writer about working-class reality
1967	P.D. James	*Unnatural Causes*	Detective stories have remained popular throughout the century

The War Poets

- If you know any of this poetry, you might be able to apply it to any discussion of conflict in a General Studies exam.

- There can be few better examples of writing having a profound effect on the consciousness of succeeding generations than that of the group of poets who described the horrors they experienced while serving as soldiers in World War I. What they wrote applies to what one of the poets, Wilfred Owen, called 'the pity of war'.

Wilfred Owen

- Owen was an officer at the Battle of the Somme in 1916, and a year later he was hospitalised with shell-shock. He returned to fight in France and died one week before the end of the war. He was awarded the Military Cross posthumously. Only four of his poems were published during his life. Full recognition came later and the composer Benjamin Britten used nine of the war poems in his *War Requiem* (1962).

- Owen is now perhaps the best-known poet of World War I and one of his best-known poems is 'Strange Meeting'.

- Owen and Sassoon give the most direct descriptions of their experiences of war.

Siegfried Sassoon

- Sassoon joined the army on the first day of the war, and this changed his life.

- At the start he was enthusiastic and was awarded the Military Cross. However, his experiences in the trenches turned him into a pacifist.

- His early poems talk of the qualities that war brings out in men, but later he wrote only of the bitterness and horror of war. One of his most famous poems is called 'How To Die'. He also compared the lives of the soldiers with those who controlled the war – 'guzzling and gulping in the best hotel'.

- After the war he became involved in pacifist politics and died aged 81.

Robert Graves

- Graves was a classical scholar and poet. His first volume of poetry (published in 1917 and entitled *Fairies and Fusiliers*) recounts his war experiences, but he is perhaps best known for his satirical military memoir, published in novel form in 1929, entitled *Goodbye To All That*.

Rupert Brook

- Brook was posted with the Royal Naval Division in 1915 to the Dardanelles and died (whilst not on active service) of blood poisoning in Greece aged 28.

- Shortly before his death, his book *1914 and Other Poems* was published which showed a rather romantic patriotism. However, it was in letters and other writings that were published after his death that his views on the tragedy and waste of war were made plain.

Examiner's Tip

The messages of the War Poets are political as well as artistic and can be used with good effect in many arguments on the rights and wrongs of military conflict, as well as in discussing major poetry of the twentieth century.

Twentieth-century music

- Just as is the case with literature, music is not just a source of entertainment. It can also at times carry social or political messages that affect many people who listen to it.

- In classical music, one of the most popular pieces of the last century was *The Planet Suite* by Gustav Holst – a series of musical pieces written in 1916 and reflecting the characteristics of the gods after whom the planets are named. The often discordant and staccato 'Mars' reflects the newly mechanised horror of World War I (when tanks were first used), while 'Jupiter' is depicted in an upbeat, jolly music – which was later used for the hymn and nationalistic song, 'I Vow To Thee My Country'.

- Jazz was a form of music that caught the popular mood in the years after World War I, when it developed around Chicago. The music was almost exclusively played by black musicians, and many bands and musicians went on to achieve world-wide fame – for example, Louis 'Satchmo' Armstrong.

- However, in social terms it did very little to further social equality between black and white. Indeed, when 'pop music' eventually emerged as a form in its own right, the rock-and-roll that had developed from jazz was rejected by some as 'nigger music'.

- Pop developed in its own right, particularly after the 1960s when British groups like The Beatles and The Rolling Stones, and US groups like The Beach Boys and singers such as Bob Dylan, elevated pop to a level some now consider to be a serious art form.

- Another form of music that has been popular since the 1920s has been the musical, perfected as an art form by Rogers and Hammerstein in the 1940s.

- Musical shows provided an escapist glamour and glitz in a time of hardship and deprivation. However, by the 1960s the spectacle had been replaced by serious, even sombre themes.

- A classic work of this latter period was *Hair* – a tribute to hippies who resisted the call-up for the Vietnam War. For a generation of young people on both sides of the Atlantic the show represented a powerful political message using a pop medium.

- In Britain since the early 1980s, maybe declining social and economic prosperity saw a return to lavish escapism, particularly in the works of people like Sir Andrew Lloyd-Webber (e.g. *Cats* in 1982, *Phantom of the Opera* in 1988).

- Such works proved enormously popular and led to continued popularity for musicals during the 1990s (for example, *Les Miserables* and *Miss Saigon*).

Dance

- Ballet is another art form popular throughout the twentieth century and has sometimes caused political controversy – for example, the Labour Government giving National Lottery money (largely provided by less well-off people in society) to support ballet, which many see as an élitist art form.

- Emerging from the ballet tradition has come Modern Dance – perhaps most notably demonstrated in the UK by the Ballet Rambert.

Important illustrations of music during the twentieth century

Year	Composer	Title	Notes
1916	Gustav Holst	*The Planet Suite*	
1930	Edith Piaf	many	French singer, first appeared in cabaret
1935	George Gershwin	*Porgy and Bess*	The first opera written for a cast of black actors
1935	Fred Astaire	*Top Hat*	The film that became synonymous with Ginger Rogers and with dance routines
1936	Sergei Prokofiev	*Peter and the Wolf*	Soviet composer who went on to world acclaim
1948	Cole Porter	*Kiss Me Kate*	Classic musical based on one of Shakespeare's plays
1950s	Pop music emerges from the music of American blacks		
1962	Paul McCartney/ John Lennon	*Love Me Do/ She Loves You*, etc.	The birth of a new era

Architecture in the twentieth century

The influence of architecture on society

- Styles in architecture affect both domestic dwellings that we live in and other buildings great and small, that we see around us.

- Architecture affects each one of us in a very personal way, such as the **aesthetic**, (which is what this chapter is looking at) or the **sociological** (for example, the effects of living on some of the huge municipal housing estates).

- Politics has also influenced building and architecture, with the growth of socialism leading to a belief that everyone had a right to decent standards of accommodation.

- Dramatic changes, mirrored in society at large, have taken place in architectural style. Today's buildings use materials that were not even invented 100 years ago.

- Important features of the changing face of architecture in the twentieth century are:
  - buildings today feature **mass production** rather than individual craftsmanship
  - architects of great buildings now have new masters – no longer is it mainly government, local councils and wealthy patrons commissioning buildings; today the great buildings are those **commissioned by international corporations**
  - the twentieth century saw the development of 'housing for all' and of 'amenity complexes', such as huge shopping or leisure complexes (increasingly situated away from town centres as more and more people own cars).

- There are well-known examples of large indoor shopping centres – e.g. Meadowhall in Sheffield – but try to think of any local developments in your area.

- **Industrialisation** in the nineteenth century led to the need for new kinds of buildings, and then the **rapid growth of towns** led to the pressure to build upwards (i.e. blocks of flats).

- **Technological development** led to dramatic changes in construction and huge visual differences. Perhaps most notable was the development of the steel-framed building, which meant that:
  - **walls no longer took the weight of the building**, so could be more decorative, or could give way to much larger areas of glass
  - **buildings could go much higher**, wrapped safely round their metal frame
  - the **invention of the lift** by Otis in the 1890s also meant that the height of a building was no longer limited by how many stairs its occupants could climb
  - reinforced concrete became a popular building material: because it was cheaper and more flexible, it allowed greater variation in design.

- Aesthetics and technological developments combined to create many of the striking buildings of the last century, which got higher and higher as the century progressed – culminating in buildings such as the Sears Tower – and used increasing amounts of glass.

- Architecture is not only about houses and commercial buildings. Think also of modern church design, such as Coventry Cathedral, or the Roman Catholic cathedral in Liverpool. Do you have any other local examples?

Examiner's Tip

Look at buildings from an artistic and innovative perspective. You might have some good examples near you – a commercial building, theatre, etc. Try to describe it in terms of how well it works.

Notable styles and architects of the modern era

- Until the latter part of the nineteenth century buildings were mainly historical in style. Some of the great municipal town halls used columns to support them that could have come from ancient Greece, for example.

- The 'Arts and Crafts Movement'. This was an aesthetic movement that influenced architectural style. Often delicate, and increasingly decorative, the style influenced the work of architects such as:

- **Frank Lloyd Wright** (1867–1959), who started his studio in Chicago in 1889. He was influenced early on by the Arts and Crafts Movement, but he also loved Japanese styles. He developed the 'Prairie Style' of modular housing, and also designed galleries and churches now considered classic.

- **Edwin Lutyens**, a flamboyant English designer (1869–1944). Lutyens was famous for his country houses, such as Orchards and Musteed Wood (both in Surrey) – although World War I virtually ended the demand for these as the 'traditional families' lost power and at least part of their wealth. Lutyens loved the rural style, and believed in trying to develop village style into urban development.

Art Nouveau

- This style became popular at the very end of the 1800s and in the years up to the start of World War I. As a style it tried to cut links with the past, and used long, curving lines – often based on sinuous plant forms, with a strong element of fantasy.

- The best surviving examples are probably the entrances to many Paris metro stations.

- The style, both in architecture and in pure art, helped pave the way for modern architecture and art. Charles Rennie Mackintosh is the best remembered British architect of the style – his Glasgow Art School (1898) is still considered a masterpiece.

- Since the style was individualistic, it was not suited to mass production, and became increasingly expensive. Art Nouveau failed to outlive World War I as a popular form of architecture.

Art Deco

- Sky-scrapers first appeared in the United States at the end of the 1800s – the first being the Wainwright Building in St Louis (1890–91).

- The Chicago School of Architects set out to erect high buildings (helped by steel framing and the lift, as mentioned above).

- These buildings often contained elements of Art Deco – an architectural style noted for its symmetrical designs which were intended for use, rather than for beauty, and which were adapted to methods of mass production. The style is noted for its curves, lines, points and stylised natural forms, and followed the demise of Art Nouveau. Classic examples, known the world over, are:
  - the Chrysler Building (1930)
  - the Empire State Building (1931), 381 metres high and perhaps immortalised in the film *King Kong* in the 1930s.

(Continued next page)

Notable styles and architects of the modern era

The Bauhaus

- This movement comprised a group of mainly German architects and designers. Based in Weimar in 1919, it moved to Dessau in 1926.

- It was founded by **Walter Gropius**, who was increasingly hounded by the Nazis in the 1930s, and eventually forced out of Germany. He then moved to the US to carry on his work.

- The style used increasing amounts of steel, glass and concrete, seeking to **exploit mass-production materials**.

- In the late 1920s **social responsibility** became important to the school – they demonstrated low-cost housing in Berlin and Frankfurt and developed cheap and popular house contents, such as chairs made from plywood.

- In 1932 a book called *The International Style* led to the naming of this type of design being popularised at the Bauhaus as 'International'.

- The Nazis hated the ideals of those working at the Bauhaus – they considered them to be left-wing radicals. In 1932 the Bauhaus buildings were ransacked with covert Nazi support. The group tried to start again in a disused factory in Berlin, but this was raided by the police and closed for good.

- The leaders of the Bauhaus joined the exodus of artists and intellectuals from Nazi Germany as Europe slid towards war in the 1930s. This provides a sad example of how an attempt to show social responsibility can become entwined and strangled by the evil of fascism.

Modernism

- This was another style popularised in the 1930s. Sometimes looking quite stark and brutal, the style made frequent use of **modern methods** and the use of **materials such as reinforced concrete**.

- This enabled the construction of **quick, cheap housing** which was much needed at the time.

- Le Corbusier is the best-known exponent of this style. Born Charles-Edouard Jeanneret (1887–1965), some of his fantastic schemes still capture the imagination of people to this day.

- He urged that people should abandon traditional cities and move out to fantastic sky-scrapers, regimentally built in vast parks.

- His dream was never realised (perhaps could never be realised), but smaller scale examples of his work survive to this day. A good example of Le Corbusier's work can be found in working-class housing in large blocks of flats in Vienna.

Post-modernism

- This style flourished from the mid-1960s, in part as a reaction to 'brutalism' in design and the large-scale use of concrete in buildings.

- Post-modernist buildings began to take on a **flamboyance**, looking light and airy – sometimes so open that infrastructure pipework and ducts are all exposed to the eye.

- Examples of this style are:

  - the Pompidou Centre designed by Richard Rogers (an English architect), the arts centre in Paris that opened in 1977, and which is constructed in steel and glass

  - the A T and T Building in New York (1984) with its Greek-style pediment to top the building

  - London's Canary Wharf and, just over the river, The Dome built to celebrate the new millennium.

Restoration

- This style has also proved popular in the years since the 1970s. You can probably think of examples of large buildings that have been **transformed for new and current use**.

- A good example that will be known to many young people will be the chain of Weatherspoon pubs, often created within the shells of buildings that had previously been banks, cinemas or had a range of other uses.

- There are also some good examples of new buildings constructed in the style of historic buildings – perhaps none better than The Globe Theatre – the reconstruction of Shakespeare's original theatre on London's South Bank.

Examiner's Tip

Try to look carefully at buildings in your locality – see if you can place them into any of the styles described here. You will see them in a different light now.

Progress check

1 Which of the War Poets died one week before the end of World War I?

2 What is the title of John Osborne's 1956 play that gave rise to the phrase 'Angry Young Men' to describe young radical authors?

3 Which piece of music has a section dedicated to Mars, the bringer of war?

4 What form of entertainment was popularised by Rogers and Hammerstein?

5 Ballet Rambert are a British group specialising in what form of dancing?

6 How is the architect and designer Charles-Edouard Jeanneret better known?

7 What school of design was based at Dessau?

8 What development in building technology meant that walls no longer had to hold the weight of a building?

9 Which British architect designed the Pompidou Centre in Paris?

10 What is the name of the London theatre that is a replica of Shakespeare's original?

Answers on page 88

Media and communication

Newspapers

- A large majority of British adults read a daily paper.
- Newspapers are broadly categorised into two groups – **tabloid** and **broadsheet**, the names given to the sizes of the paper used in their printing.
- Tabloid papers include *The Sun*, *The Daily Mirror* (the biggest sellers) and *The Mail*.
- Broadsheet papers include *The Times*, *The Daily Telegraph* and *The Guardian*.
- With the exception of *The Independent* (which lives up to its name) all UK newspapers support one of the political parties.
- Those supporting the **Conservatives** include *The Mail*, *The Express* and *The Daily Telegraph*.
- **Labour** support comes from *The Daily Mirror*, *The Guardian* and (since the last General Election) *The Sun*.
- Newspapers influence their readers through a variety of techniques, most notably:
  - **editorials**, which are articles written by the editor, setting out the views of the newspaper
  - **news stories**, which are given prominence if favourable, or are slanted in a particular way
  - **cartoons** – there is a long history of political cartoons in Britain
  - **articles** – sometimes written by prominent politicians
  - **letters** – usually supporting the 'party line'
  - **photographs** – powerful images to reinforce messages.
- Often a newspaper offers a general political perspective, but on occasions it might run a specific campaign around an issue – e.g. *The Sun* campaigning against the Euro.

Limits on press freedom

- There are some statutory (legally binding) limits on the press, together with some voluntary limitations.
- The main **legally binding limitations** are:
  - The Official Secrets Act
  - The Obscene Publications Act
  - The Contempt of Court Act.
- **Voluntary limits** include:
  - the Press Complaints Commission **Code of Practice** (established and run by the industry)
  - **'D-notices'**, which are government requests that a particular story (often of a military nature) is not published
  - temporary **'news blackouts'** on a story when the police request it to ensure their work is not jeopardised.
- Censorship does not form a normal part of press life in the UK, but in times of war information is very carefully controlled, and released through special briefings.

Examiner's Tip

While you should be aware of the press generally, reading the contents of the broadsheets will far better prepare you for a General Studies exam.

Broadsheet v Tabloid

- The **broadsheet** newspapers:
  - are **bigger**, making them more difficult to read in a confined space
  - offer **detailed analysis and description**
  - have **specialist reporters** covering specific areas, such as science or the arts
  - use **headlines** that are designed to **give insight** into the story that follows
  - provide **specialist supplements** on a regular basis, which are often a vehicle for specialist advertising.

- The **tabloid** newspapers:
  - are **smaller**, more easily read in crowded spaces like buses or trains
  - have **brief stories** and articles that are quickly read
  - contain stories that often **focus on celebrities**
  - feature **large photos**, often on the front page, that catch the eye
  - use **puns in headlines** to attract attention, or amuse
  - follow a **regular layout**, so readers know where to look for a feature
  - are often very **nationalistic**, particularly in support of national sports teams (though virtually always male sports)
  - are **cheaper** to buy than broadsheets.

- It is sometimes claimed that there should be tighter regulation of the tabloids because:
  - they print **damaging stories** about famous people
  - they treat people, especially women, in a **demeaning** way
  - they reduce complex stories to a **very simplistic** level, often based on individuals involved
  - they are often **jingoistic**
  - they create an impression that **youth** is the most important thing.

- However, it has to be remembered that **tabloids**:
  - are far **more popular** than the broadsheets
  - argue that photographs of scantily clad women are **fun** and **not demeaning or exploitative**
  - claim they are **meeting a need for 'light'** news and popular entertainment
  - rightly say that people are not forced to buy them – they are **meeting a market demand**.

Examiner's Tip

Think carefully about the appeal of the tabloids – they sell far more copies than broadsheets. Try to analyse the reasons for this and refrain from mere academic snobbery!

Television

Development of television in Britain

- The BBC was formed by amalgamating separate competing radio stations in 1922. The first TV trials were halted by the onset of World War II, so the first national TV came in 1946.
- The number of TV sets rocketed after the coronation of the Queen in 1953 – an event that most people managed to watch on someone's set.
- Independent television (ITV) appeared in 1956, but at its official switch-on time it failed to match the size of the audience for *The Archers*, broadcast on radio at the same time.
- The Pilkington Committee recommended the setting up of BBC 2, which first broadcast in 1964.
- The second ITV channel, Channel 4, followed in 1982.
- These two new stations were seen as a way of catering for minority tastes and for 'quality' broadcasting.
- Sky television was launched in 1989 – its signals being broadcast from a satellite.
- Important questions arise from the concentration of global broadcasting in the hands of a few **media barons**, such as Rupert Murdoch.
- However, it is true that recent and continuing developments, such as cable and digital TV, means that people now have a **wide choice of channels** and can watch programmes from around the world.
- However, it is claimed by some that the main effect of more and more stations seeking to attract the same number of viewers is the **'dumbing down'** of television.

The funding of British television

- Traditionally the BBC gained most of its income from the sale of TV licences, the price being set by the government.
- Today this is vastly supplemented by the sale of programmes to foreign TV companies and from the sale of BBC merchandise – books, videos, etc.
- Independent companies receive their income from broadcasting advertisements. The bigger the audience the greater the charge – hence the importance of the 'ratings war'.

Soap operas

- The battle for viewers is particularly well seen in soap operas.
- The name originated in US television, where soap companies sponsored light, popular programmes attracting mass audiences, mainly women, in order to advertise their soap powders.
- The leading UK soaps are *Coronation Street* (ITV) and *East Enders* (BBC).
- As the 'battle of the soaps' – and the need to win the ratings war – have hotted up, so have the numbers of hours of broadcasts.

(Continued next page)

Television

- There are similarities between the two programmes:
  - both are set in 'typical' **working-class communities**
  - a lot of action takes place in the **pub** – which **acts as a focus** where characters can be brought together
  - both feature characters with **strong regional accents**
  - amazing **numbers of incidents** occur in a small area
  - every episode ends with an **incident that entices you** to watch the next episode.
- However, *East Enders* scripts tend to be more serious, even violent, and tackle more **issues of social concern.**

Examiner's Tip

If you write about television, especially soap operas, be objective – no academic snobbery, nor-subjective adulation!

Progress check

1 What names are given to the two sizes of newspapers?

2 Which is the only British paper that does not support any political party?

3 Name a newspaper that supports the Labour Party.

4 In what ways do newspapers seek to influence our views?

5 What laws impose limits on what newspapers can publish?

6 What historical event led to many people buying televisions for the first time?

7 Which Government report led to the establishment of BBC 2?

8 What channel was set up in 1989?

9 Traditionally, what has been the basis for funding the BBC?

10 Why are soap operas important to the TV companies?

Answers on page 89

The nature of science

- Sciences can be divided into
  - **physical science** (physics, chemistry, astronomy)
  - **life science** (biology, botany, zoology)
  - **earth science** (geology).
- Physical science can be subdivided into **mechanics, physical and bio-chemistry, cosmology**, etc.
- Life science can be subdivided into **physiology, anatomy, mycology, ornithology**, etc.
- Earth science can be subdivided into **palaeontology, seismology, geophysics** and **geochemistry, palaeobiology**, etc.
- However, there are often **direct links** between two or more groups, e.g. the identification of DNA involved work in both biology and chemistry.
- The applied sciences are areas where scientific knowledge is used in a way that is of **direct practical use**.
- Examples include **metallurgy, electronics** and **aeronautics** (applied physical sciences), and **medicine** and **agronomy** (applied life sciences).
- The word 'science' derives from the Latin *scientia* – 'to know'. It denotes a systematised knowledge arising from the organisation of **objectively verifiable evidence**.

Scientific methods

Models

- Physical sciences try to produce **models** (paradigms) **to explain processes** that vary in size from microscopic to enormous.
- Calculation involving applied mathematics helps make physical theories precise and comprehensive.

Experiments

- Scientists often seek to build theories supported by specially designed experiments. Experiments can be used to test a **hypothesis**.

Scientific thinking

- There are two types of thinking that scientists use when trying to prove or disprove a hypothesis – **deductive** and **inductive** thinking.
- Deductive thinking is a line of thought in which all its premises are true, so that a valid conclusion must also be true, e.g. all humans are mammals, all mammals have livers, therefore all humans have livers.
- Inductive is where a conclusion goes beyond the information contained in the premise, and is at the heart of much scientific thinking.

- We can assume things will have the same outcome time after time, but this cannot be proven to be the case.

- Before the discovery of Australia it would have been argued 'all observed swans have been white, so all swans are white' but then it was found that in Australia they are black!

- To **deduce** is to use reasoning **from given facts**, to **induce** is to use reasoning **from particular cases** to come to general conclusions.

Examiner's Tip

In a General Studies exam you are likely to be asked how science and scientific method have benefited the world – so try to think of some practical illustrations to use.

Important developments in the history of science

Matter

- **17th century** The idea that small moving particles can explain chemical reactions. Newton describes how minute particles can attract and repel.

- **18th century** Researchers study heat and newly discovered gases.

- **19th century** Modern chemical idea of elements and compounds made from atoms and molecules. The Periodic Table. Emergence of chemical industries.

- **20th century** Some of the developments include: harnessing x-rays for medical use; mass production of radios and TV; plastics; nylon and other synthetic fibres; work on atomic structure – first protons and neutrons, then quarks; medical advances on many fronts; nuclear energy.

Energy

- **17th century** Experiment and maths at the heart of scientific work. Publication of the Theory of Gravity.

- **18th century** First electrical experiments (using Leyden jar); first commercial steam engines for pumping; invention of first battery.

- **19th century** Wave theory of light; magnetic forces used for making a dynamo (for generating electricity); the 'Railway Age'; machines and mechanics become ever more important; creation of radio waves; public gas and electricity networks transform home and factory.

- **20th century** Theory of Relativity; quantum mechanics; study of radio-activity; faster-than-sound travel; the 'Space Race'; increasing stress on developing environmentally-friendly power.

Natural World

- **16th century** Theory that the Earth moves around the Sun.

- **17th century** Invention of the telescope; Laws of planetary motion; measurement of the moon's orbit.

- **18th century** Halley predicts the return of a comet; emergence of meteorology; scientific journeys around the world; map of the stars; discovery of Uranus.

- **19th century** Developments in geology; first suggestion that the Earth has been changing over time; discovery of radioactivity.

- **20th century** Development of huge telescopes and eventually the Hubble Telescope in outer space; further evidence of continental drift; discovery of Pluto; study of distant universes; accurate weather forecasting; black holes.

Living things

- **17th century** Dissection of human bodies; discovery of circulation of blood and role of heart.

- **18th century** Classification of plants and animals; first suggestions that living things change over time.

- **19th century** Publication of *Origin of Species*; work on cells as the basis of plant and animal life.

- **20th century** Modern genetics, development of biochemistry and molecular biology; DNA; genetic engineering.

Examiner's Tip

The developments outlined here are only a bare outline – try to think of other examples of how science has transformed the world over the last few centuries.

Progress check

1   What are the three areas into which science can be divided?

2   Physiology and ornithology are sub-divisions of which branch of science?

3   How do scientists seek to test hypotheses?

4   What name is given to the type of thought that leads to the development of a conclusion that goes beyond the information in the premises?

5   In which century was the Periodic Table devised?

6   In the eighteenth century, what development enabled water to be pumped from deep mines?

7   Who first said that the return of comets could be accurately forecast?

8   Name the telescope that sends back images from outer space.

9   In which century was the circulation of blood first discovered?

10 What branch of genetics is creating such contemporary controversy in food production?

Answers on page 89

Our changing lifestyle

- Over the last half century we have developed the ability to **save the lives** of many sick people with better healthcare, but also to **destroy all of humanity** with our weaponry.

- It could also be argued that scientists are 'playing at God' by 'interfering' with nature, in genetic engineering for example.

- While much scientific and technological development has aimed at improving our ways of life, in the long term there is the possibility of pollution and global warming being a major threat to life.

- Science and technology are not evenly distributed – they belong to the rich, advanced economies and are helping to create an ever-widening gap with the underdeveloped economies.

Positive benefits of science and technology

- We are now **better fed, housed** and **educated** than at any time in our history.

- **Medical advances** make some illnesses, like measles, that were once killers into increasingly uncommon inconveniences.

- **Global communications and travel** have become almost routine – we expect to see live TV pictures from around the world.

- **Satellite technology** has opened up huge possibilities for:
  - education and distance learning
  - understanding global weather patterns
  - monitoring pollution and damage to the ozone layer
  - global communication – TV, radio and telephone.

- We make extensive use of **electrical goods** to enhance our domestic lives – TV, radio, hi-fi systems, video recorders and computers, for example.

- It would certainly be argued that it is not the fault of scientists and technologists that there is such inequality in the world – that is caused by politics and economics.

Problems for less economically developed countries

- Although the benefits brought about by science and technology are available to every country, they are certainly not available to every citizen.

- Consider the reality of life for millions of people:
  - their homes contain no water, electricity or sanitation
  - many of their children will not reach adulthood
  - their medical needs cannot be met because the resources – doctors, medicines, hospitals – do not exist
  - the idea of luxuries like cars or hi-fi systems, are pointless to those who have no roads or electricity!

Examiner's Tip

Whatever you think about scientific and technological development, they cannot be 'uninvented'. Try to balance the great advantages with the potential for disaster in a rational, objective way.

Some important areas of ethical debate

The arms trade

- Britain is one of the biggest traders of military hardware and technology. The Government talks of developing an 'ethical arms policy' – is this possible?
- Arguments **in favour** of selling arms to foreign states:
  - all nations have a right to **self-defence** and must have the arms to do that
  - Britain can exercise some **moral authority** through its arms negotiations
  - the poorer countries of the world are often the most **unstable** – their long-term futures will be easier with stable governments able to resist civil unrest
  - UK intelligence services know which countries want arms for aggressive purposes so the Government can **refuse** to sell weapons to such states
  - if Britain withdraws from the arms trade **another supplier** will step in – we cannot dictate world trade
  - there is no effective example in history of a state disarming itself
  - in many states the professional soldier is intended to **maintain peace** and needs weapons to do this
  - in the UK many thousands of **jobs rely on the arms trade** – it dominates employment in some towns, which would be crippled if production was ended.
- Arguments **against** selling arms to foreign states:
  - Britain is encouraging some of the poorest nations on Earth to use **too great a share of their limited resources** on weapons
  - such countries remain **in debt** to Britain (and other arms producers), which is **morally unacceptable**
  - arming other nations makes the concept of **world peace** ever more difficult to achieve
  - military capability encourages **aggressive nationalism**
  - arms sales are a way for the old colonial powers to **retain a form of power** around the world
  - the arming of poor countries enables a **military élite** to emerge in them, who may be prone to war-like ambition
  - ending the arms trade would give the UK a **strong moral role** in the world to work for peace
  - Britain would do better to provide support to **encourage world industry, trade and prosperity** rather than supplying weapons of death and destruction
  - the skills of those who work in the UK armaments industry could be transferred to the manufacture of more **socially useful products** for the world as a whole.
- What cannot be denied is that the sale of military technology and weapons to less economically developed countries accounts for a disproportionately high level of the spending of many of their governments.
- However, it would be naive to simply say that the arms trade should stop at once.
- This would lead to other suppliers (sometimes private suppliers) filling the gap, while whole communities in the UK would be hit by the unemployment caused.
- The dilemma for the Government is how to exercise effective moral influence for good in the world.
- It also has to be accepted that the UK does play an important part in UN peace-keeping missions around the world, so we need to be able to have up-to-date arms for our own troops.

Examiner's Tip

The technology that underlies the arms trade cannot be 'uninvented'. There is no easy way in which the trade can be limited – so think carefully and seek a balanced view on whether the UK should be a world weapons trader.

Industrial and technological issues

- There are important debates about industrial and technological developments, particularly those concerning the dangers of pollution and environmental damage.
- It is very easy to say that we are creating too much pollution, that we use too great a share of the Earth's resources and we treat the under-developed economies badly – but how many of us would accept a reduction in our own quality of life to address these issues?
- Many would say that pollution in its various forms poses a severe risk to the future of our planet as we know it – yet it is usually created directly by the processes that support our current lifestyle.

Air pollution

- Industrialised countries pump millions of tons of pollutants into the atmosphere every year.

Cause	Effect
Emission of hydrocarbons from vehicle exhausts and industry	Creation of ozone through interaction with sunlight – serious consequences for people with breathing problems
Emission of carbon monoxide and nitrogen oxides by internal combustion engines and industry	Carbon monoxide is a deadly poison
Emission of sulphur dioxide from factories, power stations, etc.	Dissolves in rain to form sulphuric acid, which attacks limestone and marble – including buildings statues, etc. – and acid rain

The greenhouse effect

- This describes the way in which solar energy (Sun's rays) enters the atmosphere, but the re-emission of infra-red radiation from Earth is reduced.
- The increasing levels of carbon dioxide, in particular, mean that the Sun's rays penetrate the atmosphere, but not all the heat can then escape to balance this.
- The Earth, it is said, is slowly warming up like a greenhouse.
- Effects could include:
  - **melting** of part of the polar ice caps
  - corresponding **rise in sea levels** and flooding of low land
  - increasing areas of **desert**
  - **changes in flora and fauna** (e.g. Britain becoming more Mediterranean)
  - increasing scarcity of **drinking water** in some areas
  - significantly increased **turbulence** in world weather.

The holes in the ozone layer

- **Chlorofluorocarbons (CFCs)** have been identified as the gases destroying the ozone layer since the 1980s.
- This layer protects us from the ultra-violet light from the Sun.
- The immediate risks, which we are already seeing, are:
  - increasing risk of **sunburn** if we are unprotected
  - increasing levels of **skin cancer**.

Examiner's Tip

The greenhouse effect and the holes in the ozone layer are not the same thing – make sure you know the difference.

Water pollution

Acid rain

- Acid rain is produced as a result of **air pollution** and occurs when oxides of sulphur and nitrogen combine with moisture in the air to form sulphuric and nitric acids.
- This acid joins cloud formations and might be blown hundreds of miles from where it was formed before falling as rain.
- In the early 1990s one estimate put the percentage of UK trees damaged by acid rain at 67% – the highest percentage in the world.
- Acid rain formed by UK industries has also had serious effects in Scandinavia – 20 000 lakes in Sweden have been acidified.

Pollution of waterways

- Rivers and canals have frequently been used as a **dump for waste products**, which in the past often had catastrophic consequences for river life.
- Today much has been done to end this – the Thames, which in early Victorian times was an open sewer, now has salmon and other fish in it again, for example.
- However, **pollution from agricultural practices** is a major problem today.
- Farmers spray their fields with fertilisers in order to increase food yields, which in economic terms means that food prices can be kept low.
- However, rain washes a proportion of the fertilisers into water courses.
- Streams full of bright green vegetation might look healthy, but in reality the plants are depleting the water of its dissolved oxygen, so fish and other life are killed in the worst cases.
- There is an **ethical dilemma** – on the one hand there is a need to feed people as well and as cheaply as possible, but if we create an unnatural habitat sustained by chemicals can it be justified?
- Is paying more for food in order to protect the environment an option only for those who can afford it – or does the Earth need long-term protection?
- Although pollution from heavy industries may have been cut, we still do pollute our rivers, lakes and seas by contamination from micro-organisms, chemicals, industrial and other wastes, and untreated sewage.

Pollution of the seas

- We pollute our seas in a variety of ways:
  - **oil spills** from tankers have caused ecological disasters
  - **raw sewage** is dumped below the low tide mark
  - **nuclear contamination** around plants like Sellafield, which may be very small, but which have led for international calls for the plant to be shut.
- Pictures on TV of major oil spills might outrage us, but are we prepared to do anything to reduce the West's insatiable appetite for oil and oil-based products?
- We have a love-affair with the car, and many (especially the young) see speed and freedom as their right in a car-owning democracy.
- Yet this philosophy sees ever-increasing amounts of oil being carried by bulk tanker. If we cut the maximum speed limit for cars to 50 mph we would use far less petrol. Is this a viable suggestion?

Examiner's Tip

We often do not think about many of the consequences of pollution – consider cause and effect, and the ways in which we might address them.

The use of nuclear power for electricity generation

- The main concern about nuclear power stations arises from the fact that the by-products of such hazardous fuel sources remain potentially dangerous for thousands of years.
- The reality is that many more lives have been lost in mining coal and drilling for oil for more traditional power stations than in providing the power sources in nuclear stations.
- However, there is the potential for a very major disaster involving nuclear power – we have already seen major consequences of nuclear accidents.
- Consider the facts about the nuclear accident at **Chernobyl** in Ukraine in April 1986:
  - an explosion resulting from **human error** in one of the four reactors blew off its top
  - the **design** failed to meet that of modern Western plants – so escaping radio-active material was sent directly into the atmosphere
  - the core of the reactor caught fire and burned at 1500°C – radiation escaped in a huge plume that was dispersed by wind over much of northern Europe
  - 135000 Ukrainians had to be evacuated
  - there were at least 30 immediate deaths, and an unknown number since
  - there has been a huge increase in cancer and in the number of children born with major disabilities in the worst affected areas.
- Can you imagine the logistics of trying to evacuate people from a large area around a British nuclear plant with our dense population?
- There is another problem – the generation process sees the creation of weapons-grade uranium. If this fell into the hands of anyone who was able to make a bomb (however primitive) the result could be catastrophic.
- However, nuclear power was hailed as a major breakthrough for the world in enabling the creation of cheap power.
- Millions of people in the world have little or no access to electricity. Can you imagine life in Britain without electricity at home, school or work?
- If there was an attempt to generate enough electricity for the whole population of our planet by using traditional fossil fuel sources we would create such pollution that the Sun's rays would probably not penetrate and life as we know it would be wiped out.
- It can be argued that accidents like Chernobyl only occurred because current safety and design requirements were not in force.
- Human error, or some mishap, can be quickly over-ridden in modern Western nuclear power stations.
- Renewable energy sources (wind, water and solar power) can only produce a fraction of our requirement at the moment.
- An argument that nuclear power remains the best long-term bet for meeting global energy needs can therefore be produced.
- Is this yet another example of the rich world having the resources to meet its own needs, while keeping the poor world in continuing poverty with a lack of energy sources to meet its needs?

Examiner's Tip

When writing an answer about a controversial area like nuclear energy, think carefully about the arguments on both sides, and put them objectively. You might well be given the chance to come to a personal conclusion, but your mission is not to ensure that the examiner shares your opinion!

Progress check

1 In which areas have satellites opened up global communications for our domestic use?

2 Why would ownership of a hi-fi system be useless to millions living in the world's under-developed economies?

3 What would be an immediate consequence for some British local communities if the UK stopped foreign arms sales?

4 What name is commonly given to the process which sees the Earth unable to balance the energy it receives from the Sun, with the energy it then emits?

5 The emission of sulphur dioxide by industry leads to the creation of what form of pollution?

6 Chlorofluorocarbons (CFCs) have been identified as causing what effect in the outer atmosphere?

7 What leads to many streams being filled with bright green plants that kills other life by removing oxygen from the water?

8 Name the nuclear power plant that exploded in April 1986.

9 Why are the by-products of nuclear power generation a major difficulty?

10 Why are traditional fossil fuel burning power stations not an answer to providing for global energy requirements for the entire world population?

Answers on page 90

Science and culture

- There is a view that science and culture are opposed to one another – in a sense, that science represents the future, while culture looks to our past. However, this is a very simplistic view, and there are links between them.

- Science is, 'the branch of knowledge conducted on objective principles involving systematised observation of, and experiment with, phenomena, especially those concerned with the material and the functions of the physical universe'.

- Culture is, 'the customs, civilisation and achievement of a particular time or people; the arts and other examples of human intellectual achievement regarded collectively'.

- Much Western culture is based on our Christian tradition, and it is perhaps in its relationship with religion in contemporary society that tensions with science arise.

- This is perhaps especially in those areas of science and technology once thought of as the realm of God alone.

- Our political ideologies are also linked to our culture, but there are also links with science and technology, particularly when government funding is needed for projects.

- An excellent example of this is seen as the 'Space Race' between the United States and the Soviet Union in the 1960s.

- The Americans felt humiliated and threatened by early Soviet progress and this was instrumental in leading to President Kennedy declaring that America would have a man on the moon by the end of the 1960s.

Science and God

- Over the last century or so the idea developed that there was a clash between science and God – that one had to support one side against the other.

- For centuries various 'proofs' have been put forward to either show or deny the existence of a deity, but these have been in the realms of philosophy, not science.

- In the seventeenth century, Newton's work on gravity and the nature of the universe was taken as evidence for the existence of a divine being. How else was there apparent order in the universe?

- Science does not prove or disprove the existence of God – and if it is based on 'systematised observation of, and experiment with, phenomena' it does not try to.

- Religious belief is about faith – many leading scientists are also believers in God.

- Popular religion has, however, changed to some extent with so much scientific development over the last century.

- At one time, where there was a gap in scientific knowledge, some said 'that is where God comes in' – such a Divine Being became known as 'the God of the gaps', but as those gaps became ever fewer this view of the Divine became very limited.

Examiner's Tip

Our culture might to some extent affect what are morally acceptable boundaries for scientific work, but science and culture are not opposing forces.

Some contemporary controversies

The basis for controversy

- Science seeks to:
  - be objective and based on observation and measurement
  - remove preconceptions, or prejudgement of outcomes
  - be rational in its predictions of outcomes and not directly concerned with the 'morality' of any issue.
- Some scientists, particularly those in the life sciences working in areas like genetics, might feel that their work is severely limited by the culture of their society.
- For example, a scientist undertaking work using foetal tissue (that is, tissue from a dead foetus) might find society putting severe limits on what is acceptable.
- This might suggest that science and culture are in opposition, but few scientists would deny that the purely objective nature of science does need to have some kind of 'moral framework' imposed by the society in which it is working.
- Science and culture are, in fact, related and developments in the former bring changes in the latter, although perhaps not as quickly as some scientists would like.
- Societies that are open to change, and to self-criticism, like our Western democracies, are those more likely to accept scientific development and to fold them into the prevailing culture of that society.
- Communities that are based on dogma and creed will find it more difficult to accept change, particularly if the basis of their belief or doctrine is challenged.
- For example:
  - 1000 AD – people in Europe thought the Earth was flat, that heaven was above and hell was below.
  - 1500 AD – it had been shown that the Earth was round, but heaven and hell were still physical places.
  - 2000 AD – space research has found no physical evidence of a physical God or heaven. Modern theology stresses the spiritual nature of the divine, but science has not sought to 'disprove' the existence of God.
- Controversy focuses on developments in science that stretch the boundaries of what society finds acceptable – often to do with human life itself.
- This is particularly true in some areas of medical research.

Examiner's Tip

Do not be tempted to take a polarised view – to see yourself either as a scientist, with objectivity on your side, or as a moralist, or a religious philosopher who assumes that what is 'true' or 'right' is always rooted in the past. Always look for the balanced viewpoint in any essay you write, but certainly state your own perspective if invited.

Some medical issues

- A considerable number of ethical dilemmas have arisen as a result of medical advances.

- Often these make sensational headlines, particularly when young children or old people are involved.

- However, it is important to take all factors into account, such as the need to balance health provision with the range and extent of the services that can be offered.

- In many of the areas of ethical argument there is no right or wrong – although people who hold a strong opinion might try to persuade you otherwise.

- In some cases the two sides of the argument represent doctors and health professionals on the one hand and people with traditional religious views on the other.

- The basic area of conflict is whether humans are interfering in areas of creation that belong only to God.

- Consider, for example, whether doctors should be obliged to try to keep people alive at all costs. Should people who know they have a terminal illness that will lead them through much pain and family anguish be able to ask their doctor to end their life? What about people who, in theory, could be kept alive for years in a deep coma on a life-support machine – is it murder to turn the machine off?

- A recent area of medical advance has been in the area of human conception. For example, should women be allowed to freeze some of their eggs for later fertilisation at a time when they have achieved their career goals?

- Should scarce medical resources be concentrated on very expensive treatment that will keep a few people alive, or used to treat a much greater number whose illnesses are not life threatening, but would have quite a serious effect without treatment?

- Should medical research companies concentrate their work on developing expensive treatments for the benefit of the advanced economies and their people (who can afford to pay), such as Viagra, or should they concentrate on mass-producing cures for the basic diseases that are still mass-killers in the world?

Medical ethics

- Some areas of medical research stretch the boundaries of social acceptability – such as embryology.

- Research using embryos can currently be carried out for the first 14 days of their 'life', i.e. while the embryo is still a mass of simple cells that have no specific function, such as being the direct forerunner of eyes, limbs or heart.

- However, many people – Roman Catholics being among the most vociferous – believe that human life begins with the act of fertilisation and conception.

- This also makes abortion an act of murder rather than a simple medical technique. This is certainly an area of controversy in medicine.

Examiner's Tip

Medical controversy tends to generate more heat and light – many people hold quite firm views – but if you answer a question asking for both sides you must do just that, whatever your own views.

Genetic engineering

- This is an important area of scientific advance with many applications, some of which contain cultural or ideological issues.
- It is the process of changing the inherited characteristics of an organism in a predetermined way by altering some part of its genetic material.

Gene therapy

- In this medical technique, functional genes are provided to cells that lack that function in order to correct a genetic disorder or acquired disease.
- Some hereditary diseases have been untreatable in the past, some of which have led to progressive physical decline and eventual death, such as Huntington's Chorea, a brain disease developing in early middle age.
- Being able to correct a faulty gene holds out a real hope for effective treatment for such inherited diseases in the future.
- Genetic engineering is already used to create insulin, used in the treatment of diabetes, and in the creation of Factor 8, the blood-clotting agent needed by haemophiliacs who would otherwise bleed severely from the smallest cut.

Cloning

- Genetic engineering has led to the development of cloning – the process of manipulating a fragment of DNA so that multiple copies of an identical molecule can be created in theory.
- Dolly the sheep hit the headlines when she was created in an Edinburgh laboratory from cells taken from her mother.
- There are huge moral arguments here – particularly if human cloning becomes a possibility:
  - where does this leave God in creation?
  - could it lead to the re-emergence of ideas of a 'master-race'?
  - should people be able to order 'designer babies'?
  - do we risk creating a society where disability is again seen as a sign of 'imperfection' or 'punishment' (this time by scientists, not by God)?
- Should society give moral and legal permission to scientists to do work on changing the fundamental structure of a human sperm or egg?
- On the other hand, we might be able to wipe out a range of inherited diseases, or perhaps even anti-social behaviour traits.
- However, this could easily lead to people (presumably those with enough money to pay) being able to specify exactly what sort of 'perfect' baby they want.
- Do we want the possibility of people being able to specify that their baby will grow up into a six-foot, blond, blue-eyed genius?

Examiner's Tip

Try to sort out your own views on issues of science and morality, not to 'convert' the examiner, but so you can come to a valid personal conclusion after an objective analysis of a question on such a topic.

Abortion and euthanasia

- These two things are seen as very similar by those who see both practices as murder, while those who do not hold such a view see them as being very different.

Abortion

- This is a simple medical technique to terminate an unwanted pregnancy – yet it provokes more controversy and outrage than virtually any other area of medicine.
- The law in the UK (excluding N. Ireland) allows for abortion in the first 24 weeks of pregnancy in circumstances where the life of the foetus or the mother would be threatened, or where the physical or mental health of the mother would be impaired.
- However, many doctors and nurses will not undertake or assist in the operation, since they see it as the murder of an unborn child. This view is particularly strongly held by Roman Catholics.
- Opinion polls suggests a sizeable majority of the British public support abortion – in principle at least – even if they would not want one themselves.
- At the same time it can be argued that there is a 'hierarchy of acceptability' – for example, is abortion acceptable:
  - as a form of late contraception?
  - as a woman's right to choose under any circumstance?
  - following rape?
  - when a child would be born with a physical or mental disability?
  - when there is a risk that the mother would die in pregnancy?
- Arguments about the acceptability of abortion still hinge very much on religious arguments. In practice, if a British woman wants to have an abortion within the time allowed, she will be able to have one.

Euthanasia

- In Britain it is currently illegal to assist another person to die – this applies to everybody, not only to doctors who have terminally ill patients.
- The Voluntary Euthanasia Society was set up in 1935 to campaign for the law to be changed in certain circumstances.
- Public opinion does seem to be softening in Britain and abroad. There have been examples of doctors who were, in effect, charged with carrying out euthanasia, being acquitted of murder.
- Again there is a range of circumstances in which assisting someone's death is more acceptable than others for many people.
- For example, what if someone is in a permanent vegetative state (PVS) and might remain so for years until they die? If a doctor, with the agreement of the patient's family and the courts, switches off the life-support system, does that constitute murder?
- What if a patient is terminally ill and knows they will have to go through great pain, or humiliating physical decline, being supported by powerful and addictive drugs such as morphine? Should they be able to ask to die before reaching that state?

Examiner's Tip

These are powerful and potentially distressing areas. Treat them with the gravity they deserve in weighing up pros and cons.

Animal experimentation and animal rights

- Animals are used in biomedical and veterinary research to improve the health of both humans and other animals.
- The practice has gone on for at least a century – it concerned the Utilitarian philosopher Jeremy Bentham who said that since animals felt pain, humans had moral responsibilities to them.
- Supporters of experimentation claim that advances in medicine, for example in the fields of antibiotics and vaccines, have resulted from animal experimentation.
- Current work on the treatment of various cancers uses animals, and researchers hope this will lead to the saving of many human lives.
- Experimentation and the keeping of animals for this purpose can only be done with a government licence.
- This covers the treatment, housing and husbandry of laboratory animals, and the use of possible alternatives to animals.
- The animals themselves are well fed and looked after. A researcher does not want an animal to die prematurely before results can be obtained.
- Be careful in using emotive language to describe conditions that might not be a reality – although on occasions it is true that animals might, for example, have pipes put into their stomachs.
- Also be wary of using highly emotive language to describe the treatment of animals, such as rabbits undergoing toxicity tests.
- These were the tests when drops were put into the animal's eyes to see the reaction, and were often used to test perfumes, cosmetics, soaps and shampoos.
- However, there are now no current licences for testing in the UK. The Labour government elected in 1997 said it would not support the practice, and firms voluntarily gave up their licences.

Opposition to animal experiment

- Opposition is often based around the concept of 'freedom' for animals – since humans and animals both share the Earth we do not have the right to exploit them.
- It is claimed that much experimentation is gratuitous – the same thing being done over and over, often for students or others to observe.
- This could easily be done by computer simulation – indeed, it is claimed that computer modelling could replace much animal experimentation.
- Many opponents see themselves as defenders of animal rights, since the animals cannot defend themselves. Some are prepared to go to extreme lengths, using physical force and threats against experimenters.
- Opponents also point out that because a drug has a certain effect on an animal it may not have the same effect on a human. They point to the fact that thalidomide had no side effects on animals, but terrible effects on pregnant women.

Examiner's Tip

Beware the 'poor little bunnies' argument – we are talking about the potential for saving human life here, and the quality of arguments both for and against animal experimentation needs to be treated seriously.

Progress check

1 Give an example of political ideology giving an impetus to scientific and technological research.

2 Whose work on gravity and the planets was seen as providing evidence for the existence of God in the seventeenth century?

3 What was the name given to the idea that God could be found in the areas where science did not have answers, popular around the 1940s and 50s?

4 For how long in the 'life' of a foetus is it possible to use it for medical research?

5 What group of diseases might become treatable through gene therapy?

6 What name is given to the process of manipulating a fragment of DNA so that multiple copies of an identical molecule can be created?

7 What is the basis of the Roman Catholic objection to abortion?

8 What name is given to the right to die when someone has, for example, an incurable terminal illness?

9 Which two broad areas of research use animals?

10 Why is the toxicity test no longer a live political issue in the UK?

Answers on page 90

Mathematical reasoning

- The application of number and mathematical reasoning forms part of all AS Level General Studies exams, and could help you gain a Key Skills qualification in this area if you are also studying them as part of your school or college course.
- The different Boards that set a General Studies AS Level exam cover some or all of the following in their specifications:
  - the layout of **data sets**
  - **amounts and sizes:** units, area, volume, diagrams, perimeter
  - **scales and proportion:** axis, graphs, ratio, charts
  - **statistics:** mean, median, mode, distribution, probability
  - **formulae:** percentages and rates, equations, sampling.

Data sets

- Data is 'a group of known, given, or ascertained facts, from which inferences or a conclusion can be drawn'.
- A data set is a way of setting out information in a way that makes analysis possible. Data is arranged into rows or columns so that information can be read off.
- In the exam you might be presented with a table of information from which to draw information, very possibly going on to use this data in a different way, such as the construction of a graph.

Amounts and sizes

- This covers the subjects of units, area and volume. It could include Pythagoras' theorem.
- The idea of units as a standard measure is not uncommon – for example, you may be familiar with the measurement of alcohol by units – a half pint of beer, a glass of a spirit, or a glass of wine are all one unit, they contain the same amount of alcohol so can be measured against each other.

Area

- This is concerned with measurement of a surface. For a rectangle (which includes squares) you multiply two adjacent sides to find the area:

  e.g. 4 cm $\times$ 2 cm = 8 cm^2 (squared centimetres).

- A triangle represents half a rectangle, and so can be calculated by dividing the length times the height by two:

  4 cm $\times$ 2 cm = 8 cm^2 $\div$ 2 = 4 cm^2.

- Where a shape is irregular, such as a trapezium, it can be broken down into rectangles and triangles in order to find the area.
- The ways set out above can then be used and the totals for the triangles and rectangles can be added to obtain the area.
- The area of a circle is worked out by multiplying pi by the radius squared ($\pi \times r^2$). A circle with 4 cm radius has an area:

  pi $\times$ radius $\times$ radius = $\pi \times 4 \times 4 = \pi \times 16 = 50.3$ cm^2.

Pythagoras' theorem

- Where a triangle contains a right angle you can use Pythagoras' theorem to work out the length of the third side – the square of the hypotenuse (the side opposite the right angle) is equal to the sum of the squares of the other two sides. For example, if the other two sides of the triangle are 4 cm and 3 cm, you can work out the length of the hypotenuse.

    Hypotenuse^2 = $4^2 + 3^2$ = 16 + 9 = 25
    so the hypotenuse = $\sqrt{25}$
    so the hypotenuse = 5 cm

Volume

- This is defined as the measure of extent in three-dimensional space. It might, for example, be the volume of water in a glass.
- It is calculated by multiplying length, width and breadth for cuboids.
- Where an object is a prism (a solid which is exactly the same shape all the way through), the volume is the area of the cross section multiplied by the length.

Perimeter

- The word 'perimeter' is used to describe the length of a 'closed curve', i.e. one that is unbroken – for example, a circle (where there is no gap in the line making the curve).

Scales and proportion

- Whatever exam board you use, much of this will involve the use of graphs and charts.

Graphs

- This is a diagram showing the relationship between two variable quantities, each measured along one of a pair of lines called an axis.
- Graphs are often used to show trends – for example, newspapers publish graphs showing the rise or fall in the fortunes of political parties as a proportion of the electorate that will vote for them over periods of time, or showing the fluctuations in the share price of a company over time.
- A graph is an excellent way of reflecting trends over a period.
- The same information could equally be provided in tabular form, but this does not provide the immediacy of looking at a graph.
- Information can also be extrapolated from a graph.

Charts

- These are sets of numbers in graphical form. These can take several forms:
  - **pictograms** – a simple chart using symbols, each of which represents a certain quality. They are imprecise, but can give an immediate visual impression.
  - **bar charts** – a graph composed of a number of bars, either vertical or horizontal, with the same width. The length of the bars represents the number or magnitude of the quantity being illustrated.
  - **pie charts** – these show the relative number of different elements as the slices of a circle. They are clearest when the different sectors progressively decrease in size from largest to smallest as you go round the circle.

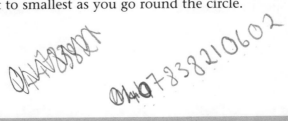

MATHEMATICAL REASONING

- It is very easy to misuse the terminology of statistics. Each term has a specific meaning and you should be aware of the correct use of them.

Mean

- The mean value is one that takes every value being considered into account.

- It is worked out by adding together all the numbers (values) that are being used and then dividing the total by the number of values involved.

- To calculate the mean of the values 2 + 4 + 4 + 6 + 9 you should do the sum: 2 + 4 + 4 + 6 + 9 = 25.

The number of values is 5 so divide 5 into 25. The mean is 5.

Median

- The median is the middle value of a group of values that have been arranged in order of size.

- It is useful to establish these when a group of values has some extraordinary values compared to the rest of the values, i.e. to minimise the effects of 'rogue scores' which could occur in any number set.

- In the scores 8, 9, 10, 11, 12, 13, 84, the median is 11 (i.e. there are three values below it and three values above).

- If you worked out the mean for the same group of values, the total added together would be 150. Divided by the number of values (7), the mean is 21.

Mode

- The mode of a group of scores is that most frequently occurring. To find the mode of the following set of values: 6, 9, 7, 8, 6, 8, 7, 6, 8, 6, 7, 7, 8, 6, 9, 10, 7, 7, 6, 7, these could be tabulated:

Value	6	7	8	9	10
Frequency	5	8	4	2	1

- It can then easily be seen that the number 7 is the mode – or modal number – as it occurs the most times (8).

- It would be easy to put this kind of information into a bar graph.

Distribution

- The idea of **normal distribution** is important in statistics. If you are seeking to establish patterns for the occurrence of a particular thing, providing the sample used is big enough (such as trying to establish the usual mid-week bed-time of a group of 30 eighteen-year-olds), and you plot the resulting times from your enquiry onto a line graph, you should end up with a bell-shaped line.

- This is because one or two of the samples will go to bed much earlier or much later than most of the group, with many more going roughly at the same time.

Probability

- This is defined as 'the numerical estimate of the likelihood of an event occurring', and involves measuring or determining the likelihood that an event or experiment will have a particular outcome.

- It is the necessary foundation for statistics. For example, a die thrown can have six possible outcomes, each equally likely.

- The chance of throwing a 5 or 6 is therefore $2/6$, (or $1/3$).

- The study of probability goes back to the French philosopher and mathematician Pascal in the seventeenth century.

- This concept is used to determine statistically the probability of an outcome that cannot be readily tested, or that is impossible to obtain – for example, if long-range statistics show that out of every 100 people aged between 20 and 30, 42 will be alive at the age of 70, the assumption is that a person between these ages has a 42% probability of surviving until 70.

Formulae

Percentages

- A percentage is simply a fraction with 100 as the denominator. 20% means $20/100$ ($1/5$).
- 'Per cent' is the Latin for 'of a hundred'.
- To express a percentage as a fraction, first write it as a fraction using the denominator 100 and then reduce it to its lowest terms:

> 25% is $25/100$ or $5/20$ or $1/4$
> 18% is $18/100$ or $9/50$

- To change a fraction to a percentage multiply it by 100.
  $1/4 \times 100 = 100/4 = 25\%$

Worked examples of percentages

- A sale offers 15% off normal prices. If a coat is normally £80, what will be its sale price?

> First find 15% of the normal price of £80:
> $15\% = 15/100 = 0.15$
> 15% of £80 = 0.15 x £80 = £12.00
> So, the sale price is £80 − £12 = £68.

- A student scores 32 marks out of 80 in an exam. What is his percentage score?

> 32 out of 80 = $32/80$
> As a percentage this is $32/80$ x 100 = $4/1$ x 10 = 40%.

- A worker's hours are reduced from 40 to 37 a week. What is the percentage decrease?

> Original hours = 40; decrease = 3
> Fractional decrease = $3/40$
> Percentage decrease = $3/40$ x $100/1$ = $15/2$ = 7½%.

Equations

- Equations that use simple letters and numbers are called linear equations.
- When solving an equation you must do the same thing to both sides of the equation e.g.

  (a) $5x = 60$. Divide both sides by 5 to give the value of x:
     $5x \div 5 = 60 \div 5$, so $x = 12$.

  (b) $3x + 4 = 19$. The inverse of (+4) is (−4), so subtract 4 from both sides:
     $3x + 4 - 4 = 19 - 4$, so $3x = 15$, $x = 5$.

  (c) $7x = 4x + 9$. Look at which side has fewest xs and remove this from both sides:
     $7x - 4x = 3x = 9$ so $x = 3$.

Examiner's Tip

If you are studying Key Skills as part of your General Studies course, the different Awarding Bodies specifications should enable you to perform at Level 3 in the Application of number.

Progress check

1 Use Pythagoras' theorem to find the length of the hypotenuse of a right-angled triangle with a base of 7 cm and right-angle side of 10 cm.

2 How would you find the volume of a cuboid?

3 In a group of numbers listed in numerical order, which would be the median number?

4 Look at the following table:

Percentage of families having use of:				
	1971	1981	1991	1993
Car	51.2	61.8	67.6	68.6
Television	91.4	96.6	98.3	n/a
Central heating	32.2	60.5	81.8	82.5
Fridge	68.8	96.1	99.2	99.1
Freezer	n/a	n/a	83.5	86.6
Washing machine	63.3	80.78	87.9	89.3
Video	n/a	n/a	69.3	73.4
(n/a = not available)				

(a) Construct a bar chart showing car ownership in 1971, 1981 and 1991.

(b) Construct a line graph using all the figures provided to show increasing use of washing machines.

Answers on page 91

Progress check answers

Society

1 Husbands returning from war realised they did not relate to their wives any more; many wives had met other men during WWII; many couples had rushed to get married in 1939 and then realised in 1945 that there was no future in the relationship.

2 Contraception; lower infant mortality; cost of children; both partners have careers.

3 Easier to obtain; marriage is less likely to be seen as a lifetime commitment; increased expectations of married life.

4 i) Accountant, architect.

   ii) Schoolteacher, pilot.

   iii) Clerical worker, baker.

   iv) Packer, barman.

   v) Roadsweeper, refuse collector.

5 a) Professionals have regular salaries; therefore it is easier to get mortgages; some professionals have inherited wealth which makes it easier to become an owner-occupier.

   b) Private health schemes; better health education; better living conditions.

   c) Less knowledge of the dangers of smoking; habit passed down from generation to generation.

   d) Increased cost and erosion of the grant system; most unskilled class leave school at the earliest opportunity.

6 **Good:** – lets the 'best' move upwards;

   – ensures people not worthy of their position become less important;

   – talent/power is recognised.

   Bad: – bad luck can lead to downwards move;

   – leads to lack of stability in society.

7 Extra qualifications are needed for 'better' employment; fewer manual jobs for those with poor qualifications; encourage, to lessen youth unemployment; being in Further Education is preferable to unemployment.

8 Budget must be balanced and kept to; marketing is done to attract pupils; need for good product (i.e. results) to keep company/school viable.

9 (a) a desire to go to university; (b) obtaining good grades at A Level; (c) need for student loan; (d) cost of leaving home; (e) wish to stay in the local area.

10 (a), (c) and (e) are free will; (b) and (d) are determinism.

11 School A is a 'better' school than B.

   School B has 'worse' children than school A.

   School B has 'worse' teachers than school A.

   Nothing, because you are judging different groups of pupils in different schools with no information to substantiate your perceptions.

Political concepts

1 Throughout history, men have held the power and thus decision-making responsibilities.
  - Women's roles were seen as submissive and geared to child rearing.
  - Women should not bother with 'this sort of thing'.

2 • The end of the 'swinging 60s' when youth first had a real say.
  - Post-World War II generations had had the benefits of higher education and were more articulate about their needs.
  - The Government of the day thought that a majority of the new electorate would vote for them. This did not happen.

3 **How:** – similarity of policies (e.g. low taxation); no real difference in either presentation or ideas;

  Why: – no longer the same class elements regarding the political parties; all parties are aiming at the same elements of the electorate.

4 **Advantages:**
  - You know how the 'race' is progressing.
  - You are aware of how people generally, or even specifically, in certain parts of the country are thinking.

  Disadvantages:
  - Polls are always dated – opinions could have changed by the time the poll is published.
  - They can be biased – questions can steer an audience.
  - An avalanche effect – everyone trying to 'get on board' to back a winner.
  - Can be inaccurate –1992 polls predicted a Labour victory.

5 Seek to influence policy; do not want power themselves; have a narrow focus.

6 **Arguments for:**
  i)   So important that everyone should do it.
  ii) Insulting to those who died trying to achieve suffrage (e.g. Emily Davidson).
  iii) Other countries (e.g. Australia) impose fines.

  Arguments against:
  i)   If someone has no interest in the political system why should they vote?
  ii) It would encourage 'spoilt papers', silly candidates, etc.
  iii) As it is secret, no one knows how people voted, so why should it be compulsory?
  iv) At present, people who do not vote cannot complain at what the government does.

7 In local affairs: by lobbying local councillors; by attending local MP's surgeries; by lobbying MPs in Parliament; can show disapproval of the government's actions by voting against them in by-elections; by using pressure-group tactics.

1   Many people do not work, e.g: housewives; young people under 16; retired people (the age at which people now retire is also dropping); those in full-time education; those who choose not to work.

Even if we analyse unemployment as those actively seeking work it is obvious that employment for all cannot be achieved.

2   Gradual reduction of large-scale employees; many redundant employees are given compensation – a large percentage of these will try to use this to set themselves up as self-employed.

3   It is the way forward: production work is done more overseas; factories are becoming increasingly automated, hence less of a workforce is required; consequently the service industry will be used to provide 'services' to the rest of the population.

4   (a) Longer holidays with pay
      – people can go further afield on holiday
      – have greater choice
      – leads to economic opportunities for those who service leisure options.

    (b) An ageing population
      – greater emphasis on relevant options for 50+ group, e.g. Saga holidays
      – greater levels of fitness. For longer periods amongst this grouping means far greater utilisation of sporting/recreation facilities.
      – a realisation that the ageing population has the affluence for leisure activities leads to service providers moving into this area.

    (c) Shorter working week
      – longer evenings/weekends can lead to employees having more time and energy to take up leisure opportunities
      – this is enhanced by the use of technology in the home, which has reduced the need for hours on housework, hence releasing people for more leisure options.

5   Destruction of vegetation; litter, vandalism, trespassing; congestion of traffic; heavy lorries and tourist traffic; wearing away of footpaths; conflict between locals/tourists; unsightly cafés/car parks, etc.

6   Cost of admission triggered by huge player wages; commercial interests dominating as to when games will be played; corporate hospitality – hence many spectators are not 'true' fans; all-seater stadia – the end of 'standing on the terraces'.

7   **For keeping railways open:**
    • they must make a profit
    • they provide a social function to the local area
    • they ensure an area is not isolated economically.

    Against keeping railways open:
    • lack of profit means subsidisation, leading to a draining of resources elsewhere
    • if not used, why should railways be kept open for emergencies?

Business

8 **For improvements of the rail system:**
- more environmentally friendly
- needs resources after decades of neglect
- other rail services world-wide receive subsidies
- needs updating from the safety point of view
- needed to ensure there is not a road 'grid-lock'.

Arguments for roads:
- the railway is not as convenient as roads
- increasing affluence means a high percentage of the population now have cars
- extra roads will ease the pressure of congestion.

9 Less based on the origin of raw materials: raw materials come from abroad; far better transport systems; far better training nationally for employees; less geographical immobility; the world is now a global village.

Culture and aesthetics

1 We have several native languages and many others brought here by new residents; we have a wide variety of religious groups – from traditional Christianity, other world faiths and modern groups and sects; history has been dominated by English conquest or subjugation of other parts of the UK – we may not have been invaded since 1066 but the fires of nationalism have never been extinguished.

2 Global satellite broadcasting; a universal 'pop culture'; large multi-national economic blocks; free movement between many states.

3 Major world faiths; styles of clothing; music, dance, theatre from around the world; cafés and restaurants serving 'world-wide' cuisine.

4 Where racism becomes part of the foundations of an organisation in an unthinking way which then, in practice, discriminates against those from different ethnic backgrounds.

5 Music – *West Side Story* or the musical *Kiss Me Kate*. Films from the 1930s to the present day, etc.

6 Lots of examples exist – 'You'll Never Walk Alone' in Liverpool; 'Bladon Races' in Newcastle-upon-Tyne, or 'I'm For Ever Blowing Bubbles' in London's East End are sporting examples.

7 'Aesthetics' is the study of the philosophy of the 'Arts.'

8 The Nazis using the music of Wagner to orchestrate rallies.

9 We can never know that others are feeling exactly the same emotion.

10 There is a need to base discussion on analysis and detail, not merely assertion of what you like.

Beliefs, values and morals

1 Judaism.

2 Church of England.

3 A Muslim school in London.

4 The Orthodox church.

5 Jesus's disciples were all men.

6 Islam.

7 Fasting.

8 Sabbath.

9 Hinduism.

10 Buddha.

11 Sikhism.

12 Marxism.

13 Freedom of the individual.

14 'Kick racism out of soccer.'

15 Socialisation.

Creativity and innovation

1 Wilfred Owen.

2 *Look Back in Anger*.

3 *The Planets Suite*.

4 Musicals.

5 Modern dance.

6 Le Corbusier.

7 The Bauhaus.

8 Steel-framed buildings.

9 Richard Rogers.

10 The Globe.

Media and communication

1 Tabloid and broadsheet.

2 *The Independent*.

3 *The Mirror*, *The Sun* (since the last General Election), *The Guardian*.

4 Editorials; the 'slant' on stories and in cartoons; letters and articles.

5 The Official Secrets Act; The Obscene Publications Act; The Contempt of Court Act.

6 Coronation of The Queen.

7 Pilkington Commission and Report.

8 Sky.

9 Licence fee.

10 They attract mass audiences.

The nature of science

1 Physical, life and Earth.

2 Life science.

3 By experiment.

4 Inductive.

5 19th.

6 Steam engine.

7 Halley.

8 Hubble.

9 17th.

10 Genetic engineering/modification.

Our changing lifestyle

1 TV, radio and telephones.

2 No access to electricity.

3 Big increase in unemployment.

4 The Greenhouse Effect.

5 Acid rain.

6 Destruction of the ozone layer.

7 Fertilisers sprayed on fields and then washed into streams.

8 Chernobyl.

9 Weapons-grade uranium is produced; the storage of some nuclear waste will need to last for thousands of years because it remains radioactive.

10 Global pollution caused would be massive.

Science and culture

1 The Space Race.

2 Isaac Newton.

3 The God of the gaps.

4 14 days.

5 Hereditary diseases.

6 Cloning.

7 Human life actually starts at conception.

8 Euthanasia.

9 Biomedical and veterinary research.

10 No firms have licences to experiment.

Mathematical reasoning

1 Hypotenuse^2 = 7^2 + 10^2

   ∴ h^2 = 49 + 100

   ∴ h = $\sqrt{149}$

   = 12.2 cm.

2 Length × breadth × height.

3 The number that is the middle value of the group of values (numbers) provided.

4 (a)

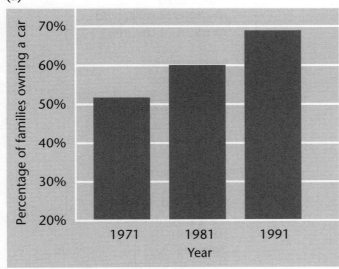

(b)

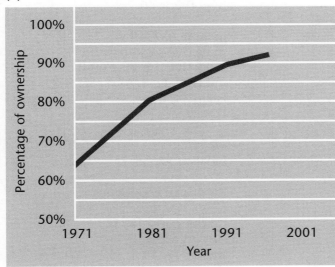

Index